The Public Gardens

LINDA NORTON

The Public Gardens

POEMS AND HISTORY

With an introduction by FANNY HOWE

Pressed Wafer · BOSTON

PRESSED WAFER
9 Columbus Square, Boston, Massachusetts 02116

Poetry/Memoir

ISBN 978-0-9831975-1-5

SECOND EDITION

Printed in the United States

Contents

The Commons

Introductory Note

Have you ever heard Dinah Washington sing "This Bitter Earth"?

Have you ever seen the movie by Charles Burnett called *Killer of Sheep*?

It was set in the Watts section of Los Angeles, in the mid 1970's and concerns itself with the fate of a family and a neighborhood. No urban landscape could be bleaker than the one presented, no series of actions more blighted, no argument for the reckless perseverance of love more convincing.

Dinah Washington's voice runs through it.

This little book, *The Public Gardens*, conjures up the experience of that movie and that song, the fate of a family and of neighborhoods in 20th-century America.

Although the title of the book shows that its ultimate point of reference is Boston, the work inside travels through New York and Oakland.

Part poetry, part notebooks, it is a model of the camera made human, made humanist, a part of arm, leg, hand, eye, a moving picture-taker pregnant with literature.

What she sees, we have all seen and passed by. But she has paused and noted it.

She quotes John Wieners, "Only the desperate go to East Boston," when her brother is sent to a halfway house there.

John Wieners *is* her brother; they are brothers in a secret monastic order of poets who see everything as it is—fallen—at the same time as they remember a day when they didn't see it that way, when they saw it as all pulse and radiance and had a fine vocabulary to say so.

The eighties and nineties in these secular cities were decades devoted to acquisitions of property if a person had the capital and the stomach (brain) for it. If a person didn't, there was just the hunt for employment, employment, employment.

Linda Norton is inevitably comforted by the spirit of the 19th century as it clings to the brick and magnolia "gardens" of the city once dubbed "the hub of the universe." The 19th century will not let go of Boston, and it is the best thing about the city, that shadow redolent of the great ones, the abolitionists, the philosophers, the poets, and Frederick Law Olmsted.

Populations who had crossed the sea to escape starvation and political tyranny have kept out of each other's way. However, they have shared religious vocabularies which are called upon, throughout this book, for meaning, for strength.

Steeped in the languages of Scripture and Emerson, the poetry here is fresh and wild, cultivated and desperate. Linda is Sicilian but everything else in her is modern. She hates what she loves. This makes her lonely, inspired, uprooted, still hunting, and blissed out whenever possible. She documents her losses and her loves, both as a free person and a mother, and every word she writes has the bitter-sweet taste of Dinah Washington.

FANNY HOWE

The greater the number of present cemeteries,
the greater the number of future public gardens.

JOHN LOUDON
Gardeners Magazine, 1843

Certainly these ashes might have been pleasures.

ROBERT DUNCAN
This Place Rumord to Have Been Sodom

Landscaping for Privacy

Self Portrait as a Meadow

There is a chair
the heart of which
is wooden
split five ways
and grass pressed flat
where we kissed
where others later kissed
on the same mattress
and solemn nothing
happening under a canopy—

Have you forgotten me?

I will go down wonderfully
as was told in proverbs
though for a long time I thought
I should not go.

Here are things that have
no Latin names
or none
that men would know.

Tomb

My tears have been my meat night and day,
while they continually say unto me, Where is thy God?
PSALM 42

At the back of the bar, where I should be safe, they throw dust in my
eyes and laugh: "Where is thy God?"

Why can't they play darts, or go to war? And leave me alone.

The Lord does not smite mine enemies, I am not vindicated, He does
not see me crying on the floor.

Dark waters to my left and to my right, pavilions of darkness—someone
shoving.
"Eat your tears and like it. That's all you're getting."

There's no escape from Latin, except perhaps in sleep, which is African
and Greek.

On my back under a blanket I dream a building is entering me. Your
building. You.

"My God."

God of stone. My home.

Trinity

First the father came in my eye,
then the son came in me
so I smelled gamey

like the tree that grows out of junk
in empty lots on Tenth Street—

tree of heaven.

I remember when
that smell of semen
came in through barred windows
at parties in summertime

and we laughed.

Now your ghost comes in my ear—
every night you're here.

.

When they come in you
they are one—

They come together in a groan,
God, spirit, man,
splitting you—

That's how they make sense.

Those medallions of bone—

One has a core of steel and pencil lead,
one is rich with marrow,
and the third is hollowed out—

So light and empty,
it's always
and everywhere—

.

And these various bones
are looped together
with a bloody ribbon
that has no end
   and no beginning

Inner Mission

This is a funny way to infiltrate a heart
    Little termite, you bore your way in

First you soften the wood with tears
    Then you go to work

Work ethic or no,
    you will do damage
    so incremental

    it's devotional

. . .

Music about music can be music
as inner tubing can be sublime
at the right moment on a river
the color of a tire

. . .

The wind came up the other day
    and tore some leaves out of a tree

At the same time a flock of leaf-sized birds
    flew into the branches

. . .

We want our trees to topple in a storm
If they sink into the ground instead,
    morphing like something in Ovid,
    our hearts ossify

. . .

The tree falls and blocks the road
We recognize this wreckage
    awesome nuisance

We can't get where we want to go
    and it's a comfort to know why

And nothing's wasted
We can use the firewood
    as we use a body at a wake

Self Portrait with a Grudge

Bow down Your ear,
O Lord, hear me; for
I am poor and needy.

PSALM 86

He took everything
though I gave him so much more.

Rose with No Name

*. . . such as are often found in old gardens growing on their own
roots, and sometimes of great age. They are of the highest value in
the garden, as the picture well shows. Such a rose, though not the
one shown, whose name is lost, is Anna Alexieff.*

GERTRUDE JEKYLL
Walls and Water Gardens

Red roses on a rose bush looped with garden hose—
The first paintings were made with blood,
beauty out of carnage, or was it red ink
from the body of the first girl, from the first
wondering about what was happening
and how it might look and how it might smell—
The heirloom roses in this garden smell old
which means they smell fresh as the first girl
unlike some of the new roses bred to blossom
thornless, fast, synthetically, to resist pests.
They smell of money and garden hoses,
pneumatically flawless, ungardened; anyone
could do it, could do them; pornographic.
The first girl, the first rose: Sapphic.

Female Form

Then the waters had overwhelmed us,
the stream had gone over our souls.

PSALM 124

Succulent typeface
  overwhelming a trellis—
Tendrils of the letter "I"—
  quaint.

I turn the page—
  here's a pool—
I should have
  brought my pail.

I lean and look
  at my reflection in the book,
wet with love,
  surrendering what was hardly mine.

Holy fool
  beyond regret or vengeance.
A fool
  is unprotected by a stance.

The lawn is soaked,
  the roses nod,
inviting decapitation—
  I'm soaked, too—

The iron gate
  to this estate—

The Public Gardens

Get wisdom! Get understanding!
Do not turn away from the words
of my mouth.

PROVERBS, 4:05

Not knowing any better
I took it for a blade of grass
and walked into poetry
in search of a place to rest,
a place to suffer formally,
a glade.

Now I am bleeding,
my mouth especially.

I cry out to tourists entering the gardens
with cameras and guidebooks,
shields and blinders:
"See how beautiful it is to suffer!
Look, I have become a rose!"

Brooklyn Journals

Brooklyn Journals

Each morning
I go down
to Gansevoort St.
and stand on the docks.
I stare out at the horizon
until it gets up
and comes to embrace
me. I
make believe
it is my father.
This is known
as Genealogy.

AMIRI BARAKA
Hymn for Lanie Poo

1987

May 10, 1987

There is a solid state, and there is liquid, and there is gas. It's the same
with the materials of poetry, you make images—that's pretty solid—
music, it's liquid; ultimately, if something vaporizes, that's the intellect.

LOUIS ZUKOSFKY, *About the Gas Age*

For me, words and sentences are bricks or food or cloth or music—they're not water. When I want water I go to the pier, the fountain, the shore, the ferry.

Joyce said that the whole of *Finnegans Wake* was an effort to make words into water. Literary transubstantiation, and the Irish writer is the priest?

When I was a senior in college, Joseph was a freshman at Columbia. I let him borrow my copy of *Ulysses* and when he gave it back to me at the end of the semester, I compared his notes in the margin to mine. His were all about modernism and European intellectual and literary history.

Mine were parochial—all about Catholicism—the intense familiarity, though we were Americans, of Joyce's Irishness, names and rituals, guilt and materials. I studied that book and *Portrait of the Artist* in a classroom at a Jesuit college. All of the people in the room were Catholic, most of them Irish. Like students in a yeshiva reading Bashevis Singer.

"My Shakespeare theme . . . 'Love sees?'"

That was what Helen was trying to teach us in our freshman Shakespeare survey—love, and ambiguity. We knew the rules, the punishments. She wanted us to know more. She came from the same working-class parish in Boston where I grew up, got the all-girls Catholic education I avoided, went to grad school at Yale, and changed.

She cried when she taught *Lear*. I remember the runs in her stockings. Much later I learned that she'd been in the midst of a divorce then. We girls were outsiders at this Jesuit school that had been all-male for 130 years; Helen was an outsider, too.

We deferred to the priests who taught us and knew nothing about girls and women. Priests who feared us or didn't even see us. Fr. Marique, who taught Latin and Greek, was openly misogynist—would turn his back to any female student who got on the elevator in Fenwick.

Fr. Shea taught the first college class I took, *Philosophy of Thomas Aquinas*. There were only three girls in the class, and lots of football and basketball players. Fr. Shea loved the boys. Mid-semester, he took a break from the neo Platonic and displayed a medical textbook filled with pictures of syphilitic sores and blind men. We girls sat at the back of the class and looked down at our desks as he warned the boys about the consequences of consorting with whores and strumpets.

I learned later that he had been giving this same lecture since 1941 when innocent Irish Catholic boys enlisted to go to France and Italy. He didn't let the arrival of women in his classroom in the mid 1970s interrupt his curriculum. If anything, it seemed more important than ever to warn the boys now that the strumpets were here on campus, right in their classrooms and dorms.

And I paid for this myself—working two jobs every summer and during the school year to augment my scholarships and pay my tuition. My womanly ideal was the Blessed Mother, a virgin, and I could not openly challenge a priest about equating actual female sexuality with filth.

Later I learned to pick the better Jesuits—Fr. Harman (philosophy of education—I first read Rilke in his class) and Fr. Donahue (Teilhard's ideas about evolution and consciousness) and Fr. Paris (who always seemed to be teaching us when or when not to consign others to death, in war and in hospitals).

We knew so little about sex. But punishment and death—I think some of us knew more about that than most people our age. Catholicism is so much about death. Parishes and big families—someone is always being waked and buried, someone is always visiting a grave. Three of my cousins died young, and now my brother is gone—and there are still dozens and dozens of us left. And at school we walked through the small Jesuit cemetery on the way to class—and kissed near the open graves—in autumn they would dig one or two graves before the frost. They could anticipate the deaths of some of the older priests who weren't teaching anymore. Old men who had lived celibate lives, and were guaranteed to go to heaven.

This life is preparation for a good death, the life to come—if you believe that—and I guess I still do, though I think of myself as an atheist or an agnostic now. But I was indoctrinated. "Lord, I am not worthy to receive you, but only say the word and my soul shall be healed."

The quality of mercy is not strained—

Was my brother Joseph able to prepare for his death? There was no time. Death by sex, shame, rage.

Joseph—

Anguished—

Extinguished—

I listened to music in his room up on 110th Street—I walked there yesterday.

I turned 28 last week. May 24th is my one-year wedding anniversary. And on October 2nd my brother will have been dead one year. My husband is not used to death, or to seeing me wrecked.

I dropped out of grad school in California, came back to New York to be closer to my mother—and to be close to my brother, by walking the streets he walked—

Why should a dog, a horse, a rat have life,
And thou no breath at all?

June 1, 1987

I have a new friend. His name is Stanley. He works in the tiny office next to ours at 50 East 42nd Street, across from Grand Central. He is a sign painter. He is Polish. I don't know how old. Pretty old, maybe 75? But he is nimble—I've seen him up on a ladder gilding the lettering on the awning of the Custom Shop on Madison, bits of gold leaf falling onto his head and shoulders.

He is going to Philadelphia for "a reception." I asked him, kind of absent-mindedly, if his wife was going, too.

He looked at me like I was dense. "It's a reception! Of course she's going!"

He says she works as a tour guide in Eastern Europe. Works for a man named Alex who plans tours of the concentration camps. The latest thing. Stanley and his wife were in Auschwitz. He says he went back with her in March, after his daughter-in-law, an American Jew, took him to see *Shoah* and "made him talk about it." So now he talks about it.

Next week we are going to have lunch at Burger Heaven. It's a good thing, I need a friend, my job is lonely, it's just me helping the boss, who is strange. I'm a little strange, too, actually.

August 23, 1987

Since Joey died—an inability to believe I have a future—a feeling that it is vulgar to go on—to think that I could have time—when that was denied him. My mother says, "Linda, you are smart, but Joey—he was *brilliant*." While he was alive she found his intelligence and his homosexuality so— queer. Now his intelligence is invoked to put me in my place. He grows larger and larger in death while I disappear.

Listening to Ellington's "Sacred Mass" and remembering the nurse on the graveyard shift at Lenox Hill last year—coming in to keep me company as I sat next to the bed and looked at him and listened to the respirator breathing him—that's what it seemed like. He was brain dead, but the respirator was alive.

There were other men dying of AIDS on that ward, many of them alone, and none as handsome and young as my brother.

The nurse took her mask off and sighed, and pushed my brother's hair off his forehead, and told me that this was the bed where Duke Ellington had died.

My brother would have loved to know that.

No, he would have hated to know that, as he hated everything the last year of his life, spitting at people, even biting my father to try to infect him (he went home, to blame or beg, and my father threw him out; as my parents threw us all out, one right after another). He was trying to leave his goofy older boyfriend, but there was nowhere else to go—he'd lost his job after he threw one of his tantrums at work—the job he loved, editing guides to the national parks.

So Joseph stayed in Louis's garden apartment on the Upper East Side, and they fed the birds out back, listened to Lotte Lenya, argued, and planned day trips. In August Louis took Joseph to Acadia in Maine. Joseph said he wanted his ashes scattered there, on Cadillac Mountain. On the way down the mountain, they smelled and then saw a moose and were, for a moment, ecstatic.

But then they fought—Joseph fought, waiting to die—and he threw a full bottle of beer at Louis's head. Raging, the last few months, leaving a lot of scorched earth and the life he thought he'd gone to New York to begin; leaving thousands of dollars in student loans, useless vitamins, a recording of the "Chants d'Auvergne," diaries, a beautiful Irish sweater, and the shorts he bought when he was a waiter that summer at Studio 54. The little shorts that shocked me. I didn't know then what Studio 54 was. Or who my brother was.

Remembering last October on the Upper East Side, in Louis's tiny, dark basement apartment: after my brother died, Louis searched hungrily for an insurance policy my brother promised he'd get, so as to pay Louis back for providing him with a home after he was diagnosed and had nowhere to go. I watched Louis as he searched. I was sitting on the day-bed, reading my brother's notebooks. I knew there'd be heartless criticism of everyone in there, including me. Too painful. I closed the notebook right after I read, "I will be a better woman than either of my sisters," and looked up to see the back of Louis's head. Louis was on his knees, rifling through a dresser drawer. I stared at the back of his middle-aged head, and saw: hair plugs, evenly spaced. Hair plugs!

He'd found the insurance policy. My brother had ripped it to shreds. A gift from the dead, the last word—"Fuck you."

"Never for less than one day in my life have I been less than completely happy."

You would not understand what Joseph had meant if you had met him the last year of his life.

But I know what he meant.

August 29, 1987

I woke banging my head against the wall. Andrew was holding me and he took my hand and brought me back to bed. I see Joey's face looking up at me from behind the respirator. I thought he was looking into my eyes but now I realize that the cytomegalovirus in his brain might have cost him his sight. With every day comes some new realization. None of them good.

After I fell asleep I had another dream. I was in bed with Allen Ginsberg, who was clearly not sexually attracted to me, nor I to him, but our bodies were touching. And I was telling him, "Allen, you must get some condoms."

We had seen him two days earlier in the East Village after an opening at PPOW. He was sitting in a Chinese place where we often see him, reading Burroughs, as he always is, it seems. (I bet he alternates: Blake, Burroughs, Blake.) He looked up and smiled at us. It's becoming ordinary to see Allen and have him smile at us.

Or maybe he's just smiling at my husband.

September 1, 1987

Wendy and Penny's gallery, PPOW, is on a street of gutted vacant buildings. But they aren't really vacant. There are squatters everywhere. The other day we saw an old abandoned couch on the sidewalk in front of the gallery. Filthy, with the stuffing coming out. It had rained, so the couch was soggy. In the gallery, all was pristine, white walls, funky elegance.

A few days later, the couch was still there, but someone had nailed about two dozen dead rats to it, attached by the tails, heads hanging down.

September 5, 1987

My lower back was hurting, I was dreaming and groaning, thinking: I can't bear this much pain every month for another twenty years or more. Maybe my grandmother was right when she said women were born to suffer.

But women were also born to be pregnant through most of their twenties and thirties.

Andrew kissed me as I slept and I said, "Don't kiss me when I'm like this, I can't take it. Get dressed, go get me some Advil." So he did.

About four o'clock he called me at work and asked me how I felt. I said, "Not so good, but listen, today I saw a man who was eight feet three inches tall on the corner of Fifth and 42nd, right near my office, and he was surrounded by about a dozen small guys in pink silk suits and slippers and caps, do you think they are in some kind of circus? And on the other side of Fifth, the bike messengers were protesting the city's ban on bikes in mid-town and they were all carrying their bikes in their shoulders, really trim guys in their black spandex shorts . . ."

I wanted to make him laugh, to repay him for putting up with me and getting my Advil.

And to make up for the cold rainy days last spring when I would break down as I passed the New Museum and saw, in the window on Broadway, Nauman's video of the angry clown, the clown throwing a tantrum, the clown crying, the inarticulate clown. I should have taken a different route but I kept going back, I couldn't help it. An emaciated man in a wheelchair with Kaposi's lesions rolled past me one day in the rain. It's everywhere. But none of the sick men I see are as young as my brother was. Why?

September 16, 1987

Ann, my new boss, is oddly militaristic, like she should be an army general, not a publisher. She needs troops to command, and all she has is me. I am "a self-starter, pro-active, a joy"—so my recommendations said—so I don't need much direction. I try to anticipate every need. But I am afraid I am no longer a joy.

We work in a tiny office, an outpost far from headquarters in California, and we're stuck together most of the day. I can hear her barking into the phone in the other room, trying to drum up some excitement, some publicity. I am in the front office, surrounded by page proof and galleys and books coming from the bindery.

Ann says I should familiarize myself with the California backlist. Our Staten Island warehouse serves the booksellers and jobbers east of the Mississippi. I can take the ferry over there if I need a book that we don't have in the office.

Or if I want to hang out with paisans, Sicilians and the diaspora from the old country, people who never read, like my mother and her family. Joe and Sandy would welcome me with open arms and buy me a sub with all the cold cuts I mostly hate. They run the business, our sub-contractor—Abeta Book Company. Joe named it that "so it's almost the first thing you see in the phone book."

I've been out there once, and didn't report back what I saw—books spilling out of the bins, banged-up monographs and tomes about Skellig Michael and Alexandria used as doorstops. Pure chaos, no pretense. Doritos and mice, and Abba on the radio. I even picked and packed a few shipments. It was very—homey.

September 18, 1987

On Italian television, a guided tour of a disco. Women in tiny bikinis dancing on pedestals above the crowd. The narrator says, "These girls are dancing for money but also for the joy of life."

On the N train the lights were out so I couldn't read. It was crowded and completely dark. A little girl with a huge cup of Coke, almost half her size, struggled to maintain her balance while trying to hold it and drink it. A sleeping Rasta with a cap so full of hair that it looked like his neck might break as he nodded in his sleep. A compact young Puerto Rican man in plastic shoes, dwarfed by the tier of Pampers boxes he was transporting. An old brown woman with tiny black eyes, staring at me, or maybe not, it was hard to tell. It was so dark, and sometimes I am so desperate for connection and meaning, I imagine things. Like Walt Whitman. Or like the Harlem landlady in *Invisible Man*, who didn't know where she ended and other people began.

A woman sleeping on the train, drugged, making tiny amniotic movements, as if she were almost half-formed; a boneless face. Her cheeks seemed edible, possibly delicious.

September 20, 1987

A dream. We're in a strange city, in an imperial but cheap hotel, with bamboo walls. Andrew piles our things on one big bed, falls asleep on another. I go out into the streets, it's night, but a kind of interminable but busy night that doesn't interfere with commerce, and there you are! Off to the side a bit, in a street that's vulgar and pulpy with the life of the market-place. An ungodly hour, I can't hear your voice, but your lips are moving. Dead, but worse than that: you look like you are still dying.

You talk to me in a monotone and it is not reassuring. No, you're not happy there, we can't be let off so easily now that you are gone. And you warn me that another loss is in store, a big one. But before I can ask a question, before I can fix the contours of your shoulders in that space between the fruit stand and the cheap Taiwanese all-night jewelry concession, a Chinese woman leaps forward and yells, "Ghost!" and pokes at you with an umbrella. Chinese butchers come running with knives, an old man tries to hose you down, children throw a firecracker at the place you once were. I'm grabbing at air.

I go back to where we're staying, and at the bathroom sink I wash my face. When I look up in the mirror, my face breaks into shards, and underneath my face, where my face used to be, I see your face. You're gone but you're everywhere.

I wake up and realize that this is a dream set in a real place, an elbow of a street in Chinatown where we ate one night when we were both students, as in a Russian novel, and were poor. We walked all the way from Columbia to Chinatown, and sat at a table at 7-10 Doyer Street at the House of Dumplings, Home of Noodles. We figured out how much we could eat with what we had—two or three dollars each.

Another night on another trip to New York, we did the same thing, this time ending up in a restaurant in Little Italy where we ordered linguini with garlic and oil. Your hair was dark blonde, your manner effete, your nose "aquiline" (unlike mine, you noted). And I—I was inescapably Sicilian-looking, whether I liked it or not.

I made sure not to eat too much that night. "You people love cheap fried food," you said to me. As if you came from different people.

September 27, 1987

Sometimes at home, after someone dies, people will ask the closest relatives, "How is Joe?" It's kind of an accident, one they will correct if they notice what they've said. But it's also an actual question, acknowledging that a man doesn't die all at once, even when a corpse takes the place of the man. The question means, "How is Joe in you? How is Joe's death going with you?" And even, "Have you heard from Joe, and what does he say?" Acknowledging the permeable borders between the living and the dead, the transmigration of souls. Dreams.

By getting scholarships and an education and meeting "a better class of people," as my high-school guidance counselor told me I would (and as my parents feared I would), I have left that behind, have entered a world of agnostics and atheists and scientific rationalists. No one I know now talks un-self-consciously of such things. The conventions of class, careerism, and respectability have dried up something damp and fertile and weird. I am lonely without it.

September 30, 1987

> *No! The suggestion that he was gay is crazy! We used to kiss each other drunk, roughhouse, but he was never not knowing the difference between a friend and a gay. It's the most bizarre idea I ever heard in my life! Do you understand what I mean? If he was, he couldn't paint the way he did.*
>
> WILLEM DE KOONING,
> *speaking about Jackson Pollock*

October 11, 1987

At Cathy's birthday party the other night, Andrew and I talked mostly to each other, as if we'd just met and were urgently exchanging information about what we liked, what made us laugh. Cathy commented on it as she went to greet more guests, young intellectuals, grad students at CUNY, or Sino-trash, as she says: rich Chinese or Taiwanese exiles in amazing clothes. Someone brought oysters. Someone compared current Broadway musicals to their original productions in London.

Over in the corner there was a game of high-stakes nihilism going on. The winner would get to go home with the most beautiful nihilist. A young man—a boy—appeared at the door, and he and Cathy screamed and kissed. He had an earring in a part of his ear lobe where there was almost no flesh. He and Cathy enthused about this achievement, the skillful use of cartilage. Then they talked about Bataille.

I knew this guy somehow. From when we lived in New Haven, when Andrew was getting his MFA? I went up to him to ask him. Had he gone to Yale? No, he'd graduated from Columbia in 1984. Ah. I started to ask him if he'd known my brother, and he answered before I finished: "Joe?" Yes, they'd lived across the hall from each other. That was why he looked familiar. I tried to talk with him, but he didn't want to talk with me. In one's twenties, at college, one should be able to have an enemy, a friend, a lover, or, as Blaustein called it, a fuck date, without all the baggage of death. Or men should be able to have that. (Women have always known that sex can have a price your body will pay.)

What was he to my brother? I wondered.

I tried to catch his eye, but he avoided me. Maybe I reek of need and grief and death? I feel so old.

Had I seen him in the hallways of the dorm when I used to visit my brother at Columbia?

I remembered taking the train from New Haven to see Joey. I was proud of my clothes, I was making an effort to dress better, I'd gone to Filene's Basement to improve my wardrobe on my last trip to Boston.

He wasn't at his dorm when I showed up at the appointed time. I waited forever. Eventually the Dominican guard decided to let me go up to my brother's room, and he unlocked it for me. I sat on my brother's bed in the suite, reading a collection of O'Hara poems. The cover, a drawing of the poet, naked, uncircumcised, shocked me. I kept reading:

> Those features etched in the ice of someone
> loved who died

Eventually my brother appeared (now I think he must have been having a tryst, or is that too beautiful a word; no, that would have been his word). He was angry that the guard had let me in. "You are exactly the kind of girl who made the Weather Underground so dangerous! Seemingly innocent and unobjectionable."

Flattering that he thought I could be so cunning, so subversive. He glamorized my conventionality, my oldest-sister ways, my pious lapsed Catholicism and my working-class pedestrian nature. But he knew this was not a pose established in order to subvert the establishment. It was something real and stolid and unconscious, something that made me old, and I hated it while I defended it. He had nothing but contempt for what he'd left behind, and I was part of that, though I kept morphing into something or someone who might have some relevance for him. We both wrote, we cared about music, we read books, we had friends in common, the artsy gay kids from our high school. I, too, contained multitudes, even if I wasn't a gay male poet.

One Christmas he'd bought me a vintage Pucci blouse that was too small, I couldn't button it across my breasts. He was disappointed, then disgusted. Pucci was wasted on me.

He picked up the gloves I'd bought at Filene's Basement, of which I'd been so proud. For me to spend anything on clothes instead of on my education, the bare necessities, tuition—this was something new.

"Vinyl," he said, smelling the gloves. "Can't you at least *try* to get real leather gloves?" I frowned. I hadn't realized they weren't made of leather.

"Come on," he said. "Let's go." And we walked to the Hungarian Pastry Shop, where everyone but me was smoking cigarettes. And reading. I loved that part. The reading. The solitudes, and the people reading together, and talking about reading.

October 16, 1987

> Man, you will be transformed
> To that which you hold worth;
> God, if you loved God,
> Earth, if you loved earth.
>
> 17th-century mystic ANGELUS SILESIUS

Today I had an urge to play a photograph on a turntable, as if the needle would find a groove in the picture and reveal a song, and information, that we cannot see.

November 2, 1987

All Souls Day.

In my notebook there's a red leaf I took from the maple tree in my parents' front yard when I was there last month. No matter how ugly it gets in that house, that tree is gorgeous every October. When I was in high school it made me happy to walk up the street and see it, even if I dreaded my mother's rages.

If there was a truck parked outside the house, I knew she'd be in a good mood—it meant that one of my older cousins, from my father's side of the family, had taken a detour to have a cup of tea with my mother. Bobby drove a UPS truck and Frankie, a Vietnam vet, was a Teamster. Frankie had a tattoo—*Linda,* the name of an old girlfriend—that made me blush when I was twelve, thirteen, fourteen years old. He used to take us ice skating at the quarry behind the Purity Supreme.

Frankie drove a big Coca-Cola truck. He'd pull up on the sidewalk and go inside to eat pizzelli at my mother's kitchen table. We'd come home to find him laughing with my mother. There was one other Italian in-law on that side—Jackie's wife, Suzie Martinelli. She was cute, too. Marrying an Italian girl was as exotic as it got for that generation of Irish Catholic men in Boston. All the women were called by their maiden names, which was important when it came to the many Marys.

I wonder now—what did the neighbors think when they saw those trucks parked outside my mother's door for half an hour while we were at school?

1988

January 18, 1988

When we visit my parents, Andrew protects me, not by doing anything explicit but merely by his existing. He is not particularly protective—but being married to a tall man with a deep voice protects me—my mother can't hit me when he's there. He goes down to the basement and reads while I sit at the kitchen table with my mother and my aunt, drinking endless cups of tea. I know he's there, and I know we can escape if we need to.

And we needed to. We went for a walk in Scituate. Bleak and beautiful, bare birches, black ice on the marshes, and in the woods, panes of ice crackling under foot. I had just read some of my brother's late letters to my mother and was rattled. Clearly, at the end of his life, his delusions of grandeur had been intense. He had written to my mother to explain the life he should have led, would have led, if he had been her only child, instead of her having the five of us, four of us so mediocre and expendable. He would have gone to Oxford . . .

He'd enclosed a clipping about Auden, Forster, Spender, from the *New York Review of Books*.

Not in a million years could my mother have understood his references. I have never seen either of my parents reading a book, except for the AA Big Blue Book that my father got when I was fourteen and he stopped drinking. But my mother would take us to the library, and we had a few books when I was growing up: *The Warren Report*, about the Kennedy assassination, and Kennedy's *Profiles in Courage*; *Old Mr. Boston's Bartending Book*; *The Hood Cookbook* (a tome published by the old Yankee dairy for the Irish housekeepers who worked for Boston Brahmins and needed training in the New England domestic arts).

My father worked as a shipping clerk for a company that made medical instruments, and sometimes an airline would send him brochures about foreign places. I loved the Lufthansa booklet about Rio: "Nights in Rio can be chilly, so be sure to bring a light wrap." I shivered, reading that—anything about wraps or robes, or disrobing, was redolent of the sacred—the Blessed Mother, the weeping women around the base of the cross, their faces in shadow—and the profane.

I found a book about "health" under my parents' bed—it was hidden because it was dirty—there was something about sex in it, I knew the first time I saw it under their bed. The binding was falling apart and it was secured by two big elastics. I'd sneak up there, take the book out, and the pages would always fall open to the same spot—about the wedding night. The narrative was so oblique that I had no idea what sex really involved— Fear? Love? Shame? Terror? I puzzled over the author's suggestion that the husband should wait patiently while his bride "disrobed" for the event.

We also had Dr. Spock's book about baby and childcare, which our pediatrician, Dr. Djerf, had given my mother on one of his many home visits. He used to come to our house to help Ma with our epileptic brother, our dehydrated sister, the bedwetting and impetigo (I don't think she ever acknowledged that we had worms, or sought treatment; too shameful).

We were stuck on the top floor of the three-decker in Neponset during a blizzard, and Richard had a seizure. He must have been very little—three or four years old? I remember Dr. Djerf arriving—"Mother, Mother, bring me a towel"—kneeling on the floor in the kitchen, lifting the scapular from my brother's neck as he checked him with the stethoscope. Nonnie had bought the scapular at a shrine and had given it to Richard for protection from demons and seizures.

My mother complained about our "disobedience", which for her was all wrapped in our punishment and hers, our afflictions—she was afraid. Dr. Djerf told my mother that they were just kids, and they were sick. (And there were too many of them, of us, all in a row, five kids in six years. But he didn't say that.)

He left the Spock book one day, and my mother spoke of it with contempt ever after. I was the only one in the family who read it. Thus I became a pain.

January 21, 1988

Stanley wonders why Andrew hasn't yet found a job that can support us. I know he's also wondering when I will ever be able to be a mother if things go on like this. How can I explain? I just smile and nod and tell him not to worry: Andrew is an artist.

Last week he told me about the displaced persons camp in Munich where he and Susan stayed until they could leave for Palestine. Then from Palestine they came to New York where he drove them around on a motorcycle. Cute.

A few days ago he brought his old passport into the office so I could see how he looked when he was young, before he had heart bypass surgery. He looked like a provider and a protector. Virile and burly. I guess that's why he wanted me to see the picture. You can't tell from the picture that he's really diminutive, about my height, actually. He still looks like a provider and a protector though he's much thinner and older now, and his hair is white.

March 6, 1988

In the Old Testament they were allowed to feel wrath and to want revenge, and they were triumphant when their enemies suffered, and were filled with self-pity when abject, and said so.

> *I am weary with my groaning; all the night make I my bed to swim;*
> *I water my couch with my tears.*
>
> 6TH PSALM OF DAVID

The New Testament hangs heavy around my neck. When I try to turn the other cheek, as I have been trained to do, I hurt my back. I'm warped from all this dishonesty about my emotions and motives, and so are many of the people I know.

May 4, 1988

Beautiful day. Ann is in DC. I worked. I started to write a press release about yet another "superb" book that will "force" people to deal with (fill in the blank: racism, sexism, the Catholic Church's misogyny, the plight of unwed mothers) at last.

I put that aside and packed Cranes for reviewers, filled out the UPS log, and took the postage meter to the post office and had it refilled. When I came back I fiddled around with the new computer database (I'd rather type, and I think my handwritten notes sent with review copies get results).

I went into Ann's office and snooped around. Nothing intriguing in there.

I felt a little guilty that I'd done that, so I cleaned her blinds, her bookshelves, her couch. The cushions under the sofa in Ann's office—disgusting. Mice have lived there for years.

Our office is a pit. We look out onto a shaft and if I want to know what the sky looks like, I have to crane my neck against the window and look way up. And then I can see the Pan Am building.

I played the radio loud (Phil Schaap at WKCR is crazy good; and just crazy) and went out for coffee with the UPS man, Chris, who told me that our other UPS man, not a comely sort at all, was once a swinger in Texas. "No, really," he insisted. This guy had shown Chris a picture of himself naked on a couch with other naked swingers. In Texas.

We laughed so hard. I was happy.

When I came back I realized I'd forgotten that I was supposed to meet with some friend of a friend of a friend who wants to get into publishing and was eager to talk with me about how to do it. I washed up as best I could and greeted her at the door. She was dressed in heels, carrying a brief case, wearing a Perry Ellis suit. I was filthy, wearing an odd sort of smock I'd had since high school and jeans that were too tight (not in a sexy way).

When I got home I told Andrew about this absurd meeting and said, "Oh, God, the way I looked, I can only wonder what she thought."

He said, "Maybe she thought, 'This woman must be great at her work, to get away with dressing like that.'"

July 17, 1988

We are publishing the Marcus Garvey papers and went up to the Schomburg Library in Harlem for a press conference to launch the book. Ann and I were the only white people in the room. A guy from a separatist black newspaper glared at us and asked the director of the Schomburg why white people were publishing Garvey's papers. "Why isn't this work being done at Howard?" The director answered suavely, talking about federal funding for the humanities, etc. After the press conference, we went into his office to talk details and he laughed, apologizing because he felt we'd been put on the spot: "Why are we doing this work with a 'white institution'? Why aren't we doing this work at Howard? Because everyone knows no one can get any work done at Howard!"

I had arranged a radio interview on WBAI for one of the scholars who edited the volumes. He went down to the station and I went back to my office and turned on the radio. The host is one of Haile Selassie's many children. He likes our books and we get along. I've booked several of our authors on his show.

He had invited a couple of Rastas to join the Garvey scholar on the show. First the professor talked about Garvey's life and death and the challenges of editing the papers of the Universal Negro Improvement Association.

Then the host turned to ask the Rastas what they thought of the professor's comments. There was a stunned, or stoned, silence, and one Rasta said, incredulously referring to the professor's reference to Garvey's death: "Dat mahn, he tink Garvey dead!"

September 17, 1988

In the library two girls are studying, occasionally singing a phrase to help them with memorization. The Mohammedan word for Jesus, and some African grammar from an Oxford book of something or other. Singing as an aid to memory.

And a woman is highlighting in yellow various details of a drawing of a bladder, with a pen that looks like a banana.

October 18, 1988

Went to see Robert at the Algonquin. He's in town to live it up while he dies. Last year when he was here, he took me to lunch in Soho and tossed his AZT pills on the table dramatically as he announced that he had AIDS. He looked fabulous as usual in a great suit with his head of gorgeous silver hair. (My brother died the week before the discovery of AZT was announced. It has changed what is possible after the diagnosis, at least for some people.)

This year Robert is pitifully thin. He held court on his hotel couch in a short nightshirt that showed off his legs, but there is no air of death hanging over him. He's seeing every big musical, every hot play, demanding the best seats because he has AIDS. He used to be a parish priest, but he lets everyone think he was a Jesuit because it has so much more intellectual cachet, and since most of the people we know in publishing aren't Catholic, they don't know the difference.

If he ever stopped talking, we would all be depressed. But he never stops—he says the most amazing things—as an aside, he mentioned that my brother "must have been one of those early, promiscuous cases"—and we just sit and listen, and do his bidding. He is still the man to whom we report, officially, and we are deferential.

He asked us to bring him some books from the office—all the Twain we have. He first got sick after a trip to China where he was trying to make sure the Chinese publishers didn't infringe on our Twain copyright. He came home with some weird infection no one had ever seen before.

I promised to come back the next day with the books. On the way out, I saw his dirty diaper in the trashcan.

December 31, 1988

Back from the meeting of philosophy professors in Washington, where I sold books and talked to authors. So many books were stolen from our booth—what is it with the philosophers? I watched a professor put Hegel down his pants.

At Penn Station, the usual circle of hell—homeless schizophrenics making filthy Stations of the Cross, stopping at each trashcan to mutter prayers and incantations. A pilgrimage. Visionaries, like my brother Richard. Big ideas. They talk about Marcus Garvey, Malcolm X, Jesus Christ. And the mother of God, how she got fucked. Funny how you never hear a schizophrenic talking about Martin Luther King.

I came home to a message from Ann, who said Robert died on December 22nd: "I just thought you should know."

1989

January 20, 1989

Visiting my parents in Boston. Nightmare. The craziness, the screaming. I went down into the cellar to get Andrew. He was sitting in my brother's old room, the cave Joseph carved out for himself and tried to decorate in style. I sat next to Andrew and picked up one of Joey's old books, opened it and saw his handwriting on the flyleaf, the penciled words: *Hi there*.

March 17, 1989

The softness of the evening and the sky as you come up out of the subway—a blue flannel sky, worn out, faded. The beautiful woman on the F train, covered with sores. Could you heal her? Could she kill you?

Friday I was sitting at my desk, looking down at Court Street, and I watched the bag men go around to collect protection money from all the merchants. They put the money in a shaving kit, brown vinyl. The Longshoremen's Union barely exists here anymore, and the docks closed long ago, but the racket continues.

I always smell it before I see it: the enormous green tallow truck that rumbles down Court Street every Friday, picking up bones from the butchers and the restaurants. The pink pile of bones and flesh, to be rendered later, made into soap and candles and grease. No one on the street knows what's in that truck, really, but I can look right down into the mess from my perch on the third floor. Flesh, bone, blue veins. There's a big shovel hanging from the side of the truck, and a (bloody) decal of the American flag on the back door.

> *My God, my god . . . such sinews even in thy milk.*
> JOHN DONNE

I look down at the people walking along the street, I see the parts in their hair, the tops of their feet.

June 12, 1989

The Chinese woman on the F train, coming home from work in the garment factory, worms of white thread clinging to her vest and the seat of her pants. Leaving the E train at 23rd on a Sunday afternoon, I pass a small elderly man. He's wearing an artificial pink flower on his lapel, and a button that says USHER.

Porters, ushers, pall bearers: why are there never any female pall bearers? I had a dream that I was helping lift a coffin and then I woke up and realized they wouldn't have let me help.

I used to feel a rush of pity, overwhelming and breathtaking, at some of the things I would see in the street and down in the subway. Now it is more of a click, like a lid landing on its pot.

Party at Walter and Roxanne's the other night. The loft is so big, or so long, that they took out a bow and arrow and we took turns shooting arrows at the bookcase at the far end. Andrew split a book by Bataille right down the middle of the spine. He said he wasn't aiming at anything.

Later, after everyone else had gone, we sat talking near the windows overlooking Greenpoint Avenue. Andrew was talking about how hard it is for him to walk long distances. Walter said, "You? I'm surprised. You look so—Alpine."

July 2, 1989

A rich broth of chicken, the yolk of an egg beaten in sherry, a very ripe peach—

Things the nurses tried to feed Simone Weil to prevent her from starving herself to death in August 1943.

Yellow golden orange tawny ochre could not tempt her.

"Creation is abandonment."

My sister called. Says that my father is now buying huge jars of spices, canned food, boxes of cereal, and labeling everything with his name. My mother has her own labeled stash, too, which she keeps in the cellar. They are moving Joseph's books so they will have room for their food.

July 26, 1989

Ninguno es necessario
ni aun para ti, que por definicion
eres menesterosa.

No one is necessary
not even for you, who by definition
are so needy.

ROSARIO CASTELLANOS

August 30, 1989

My boss left abruptly for another job and now I am doing her job and mine. Actually, she probably tried to hint that she was leaving, but I didn't get it. I am doing trade publicity for a few books, booking authors on the radio and planning a few book tours. When I go out to talk with reviewers, they tell me I'm not like other book publicists, meaning: I'm serious and quiet. Too serious? Too quiet?

I don't know if other book publicists get excited about Rabbinical Judaism and the way Hellenic Christianity grew out of it. Today a batch of advances arrived from the bindery and I opened it with the box cutter, excited to find ten copies of *Carnal Israel*. The cover is a delicious persimmon color and the books were hot because the box had been sitting on the UPS truck on 42nd Street all afternoon. I never saw a more succulent book. I sat down to read.

December 7, 1989

Hodge came to the office for lunch again today. He brought me juice and a sandwich. Two days ago he brought me a book about David Hammons. We talk on the phone almost every day, even though we hang out with each other all the time at the studio he and Andrew share in Williamsburg. He has a really pretty girlfriend. Why isn't that enough?

We sat in Ann's old office while we ate. "But it's your office now," he said. I haven't really taken to being a manager yet. I am my own assistant until I hire someone part-time to help me here. Hodge says he will come in next week to help me move things from the front office to this much bigger, but equally dingy, back room.

We sat next to each other on the couch, staring straight ahead, not at each other, talking for an hour. He was wearing handsome new black shoes, and they looked hard, like a door. I bent down and knocked on them.

He said, "Barney's," and looked embarrassed. Shoes from Barney's cost how much? I think he has a trust fund. I used to think he was just like us, like me, but one day I saw something on the table on his studio, a brokerage statement, and then he quit his job so he could focus on his art career, which is what he does. He doesn't paint that much but he makes a lot of phone calls and knows everyone.

It snuck up on me, this intimacy. I spend more time with him than I spend with my husband. What is going on?

Fata de la gunda— Nonnie always says this to Ma when she's acting stupid—Figure it out yourself.

1990

January 28, 1990

In Chinatown, the cobbler who works in the street. His customers stand on one foot in the cold while he fixes one shoe and then the other.

A fish monger sorts through a big delivery, finds a starfish—small, alive, and maimed—and throws it in the gutter. Strange to see it undulating, dying in a dirty puddle.

March 22, 1990

The man at the library, traces of dry white foam on his lips, as if the tide had come and gone there.

After my brother died, they removed the respirator from his mouth and nose, where it had been taped for ten days. White traces of adhesive surrounded his mouth. I tried to wipe it off but I would have had to scrape it to remove it, would have had to do violence to his face, so I stopped.

March 26, 1990

In the window of the fish store, a sign:

SHAD

At once direct and cryptic, perhaps a code word, or a curse on the neighborhood.

April 1, 1990

Andrew is away. I am usually the one who goes away. My solitude quickly turned into loneliness. I called Hodge. It was like he was waiting for me to call. He said he would come over after dinner with Lisa and Suzanne.

He arrived an hour later, we poured big glasses of wine and sat at my desk, reading the Oxford English dictionary, looking for things. Celadon—prolegomena—cuppeity (which was not there)—synecdoche.

August 15, 1990

Obit: Ethyl Eichelberger died. He had AIDS, he slit his wrists.

I didn't know he was born to Amish parents. Amazing performer. When was it we saw him in one of his fabulous wigs, playing Medea in his one-man show at Dixon Place? We were sitting in the front row and he was declaiming furiously, spitting, and his spit rained down on me. I relished that dirty baptism, I was laughing and crying, like everyone else in the room.

August 17, 1990

Long life to you, o happy soul.
The Pool. The palace. The
oyster beds. The shore.
The pillars.

INSCRIPTION ON A BOTTLE,
3rd or 4th century AD, Puteoli, Italy

Walked from the Met to the Conservatory Garden. Bees, and papery or succulent flowers. Pink, yellow, orange, violet. The carapace of a beetle is stuck to a tree trunk, with a hole in its back where a bird must have pecked it. The beautiful expensive subtle color of the beetle, a Bonwit-Teller kind of color—shoes, bags, hair, silk blouses. Brittle sophistication, versus the pillowy sophistication, the inexpensive public luxury, of sitting in the sun when the sunlight seems lazy, palpable, resting on the bushes and branches, almost leaning on things.

It's Central Park, so there are rats. But just two.

August 25, 1990

My mother called to update me about the wakes and funerals they've attended this month. They go to more funerals in a month than some people attend in a lifetime. AA and the parish and the big families keep them busy. While talking to her I heard the back door slam at the other end of the line, and then she yelled: "Dick! Dick! Are you going to that kid's wake down in Kingston? Scottie's kid's wake?" I didn't ask who Scottie was, though usually I want to know as much as she can tell. (She talks so much it's almost scary, and she's always lowering her voice to warn me not to tell anyone about Mary's new refrigerator or the Greek next door, or what happened to Dad's AA sponsor's mother at Mass General last week. Who would I tell? She's conspiratorial. So Sicilian. Going into the pantry with my grandmother or my aunt to whisper something we can't even understand, since they are speaking their version of Italian.)

She sent me a "percale" sheet. (One hundred percent polyester, and Andrew would never let me put it on our bed, but because it is called "percale," she thinks it is luxurious. What is percale, anyway?) Mary Barrett's nephew died of cancer, 26 years old, an architecture student. He also liked Rilke ("Rilk," my mother says). Like Joey did, like I do. My mother pretends to believe Mary when she says it was cancer, but she doesn't believe it, and neither do I. And she would like some company and no one up there will admit that anyone but my brother has died of AIDS. At least in New York I'm not alone with it.

My mother asks me about Louis: is he sick? And what about my old friend from high school, Paul Cullen. (I told her that Paul is gay—I wanted her to know that she was not the only mother in the parish who had a gay son).

I deflect my mother's inquiries, telling her I've decided not to call them all the time, because it's as if I'm calling to see if they're dead yet. "Hi, you still alive?"

Two of the Bean boys have died of AIDS, not that anyone talks about it openly back home. Paul's oldest brother is sick, too. These big Catholic families have so many kids that sometimes there are not one but two gay brothers. All of them former altar boys.

And there are a few girls in the parish who've had some kind of sex with these guys, like Marianne, my old friend, who changed her promiscuous ways abruptly after one last horrible affair, and married a Muslim man and took the veil, renouncing or denying her old life. She came to Joey's funeral, and that day I realized that she was carrying a big, dangerous secret. She and Joey were roommates in Cambridge one experimental summer.

On the phone I recited for my mother the Auden line that Eve Sedgwick quotes in *Epistemology of the Closet*: "And death put down his book."

September 30, 1990

The sound of low, spontaneous laughter spilling out the back door in the dark—pleasure poured from a bucket—and the eventual relish of a punch line: "With this nose, I shouldn't speak Yiddish?"

October 2, 1990

Reading Sewall's biography of Dickinson. From a letter to Otis Lord, 1882: "We both believe, and disbelieve a hundred times an hour, which keeps Believing nimble."

Joseph. Four years. There may be a day and a year when his death is acceptable—Nan, the human resources lady at Stewart, Tabori, and

Chang who kept him on his health insurance after he was fired, tells me that some day I will be able to turn his picture to the wall, to move on, and she should know—

October 19, 1990

In the lobby at 50 East 42nd Street, waiting for the elevator after lunch. The door opens and a man my age steps out. He has an amazing head of dreds, volumetrically astounding. Another woman waits for the same elevator—neat, suburban, blonde, about fifty. As he leaves the elevator there is an air about her—scorn, fear, incredulity that he has business in our building. We step into the elevator, the door closes, and she looks at me, trying to catch my eye, assuming we'll conspire: "These people!" I look down, avoiding her, because I don't want to be forced to be white with her.

Awkwardness, and then her coolness, after this refusal—this distance that she'd never imagined could exist between any two white women in such a situation.

October 21, 1990

From an errata slip in the MOMA edition of Van Gogh's letters, 1938:

> Page 44   *For:* and yet relieves our despair
> *Read:* which arouses our despair

October 28, 1990

In Natalia Ginzburg's novel, *All Our Yesterdays*, she talks of a Southern Italian peasant, an old servant woman whose life is drudgery. The prince passing by in his carriage in the distance provides the only occasion for romance and distinction in her life. Whenever she sees the carriage in the distance, she sighs and thinks to herself, "There goes the carriage of my seducer."

I think of this whenever I come out of my office on 42nd Street and see the buses passing each other in the street, displaying huge ads for Forrest Johnson's latest play, another Broadway triumph, winner of a Pulitzer and a Tony. I remember when he was the cook where we worked—a poet and an aspiring playwright. He'd read every poet in the world, it seemed, but had hardly seen any plays. Now the critics compare him to Eugene O'Neill and Tennessee Williams. The hype is a bit much. Soon they'll be calling him the black Shakespeare. A race man, indeed. Must feel good. He never liked how white he looked.

Sometimes a bus with the big ad with his name on it will be heading east as another one with the same ad is heading west, and they pass each other right in front of me, and I feel very small, and I remember him saying, when I left, that it wouldn't be so easy to get away from him, that he would haunt me.

He told me he would be famous some day, would take me to New York and buy me dresses, but I didn't believe him. At that time he was mostly, to me, the cook, the man who told fantastic stories with a sparkle in his eye, playing all the parts. To have him watch me while I ate the food he made—to have him tell me stories—and tell me how beautiful I was—to read a draft of his first play, to realize with a gasp that he was *good*, a real writer, not a poseur—yes, I liked that, I admit it. The food, and the attention, and talking about books and poetry and music, and driving him home, since he didn't drive, and watching him walk away in his windbreaker and cap with his notebook under his arm. I'd never met a writer before. Or a man who could feed me. A grown man who spent afternoons resting on the couch listening to the blues, and called that work.

"There goes the carriage of my seducer." I walk into Grand Central, laughing.

November 20, 1990

Brighton Beach, Brooklyn

The old yogurt in the Russian bakery
The cat's whisker in my sherry
The cherry pastries
The man in the same place for a long time
Ravenous seagulls
The Mandarin oranges, six for a dollar, the leaves still on the stems
Russian erotica, a plump woman with big arms embracing an enormous
    man
The runner who took a tumble on the boardwalk
The noise he made when his knees and knuckles hit the planks
The man scooping lots of small cucumbers into a bag
His pickling plans in mind
The woman at the bagel place—her beautiful lips, fortitude, disgust,
    resignation
The old customer who squeezed all the bagels before he paid for them
The buttermilk we drank near the beach
The streaks of light on the water
The ship that looked like a city on the horizon
A Jerusalem of smoke stacks and turrets, disappearing
You, with rough cheeks
Walking close to the water, climbing the rocks
I recognize you by the shape of your legs
Watching you from far away
Where I sit near a Russian family of four, including a girl
With enormous ears
And a toy passport

    Shrike to Miss Lonelyhearts: *You can know nothing of humanity; you
are humanity.*

1991

January 4, 1991

Walter said he liked the way I danced at the party the other night.

> *Heavy upon me, yea,*
> *All the black same I dance my blue head off!*
>
> JOHN BERRYMAN,
from "King David Dances"

January 14, 1991

Late-night walk to Brooklyn Heights and back. I sat on the Promenade and watched two ferries cross paths. The perfect squares of light, the windows of the ferries. The prop-like qualities of the trees in Brooklyn Heights—are those sycamores?—they all lean in the same direction, as if *intending*.

Came back by way of Fort Greene—major detour. The buildings there are decadent—elegant places turned into rooming houses and now in shambles—junkies and geniuses on the stoops, and chicken bones stuck in the sewer grates. There are ghosts in Fort Greene. The foreheads of the buildings seem to brood, disappointed. Having seen so much.

I was not afraid.

January 20, 1991

Sid Mark's "Sounds of Sinatra." I used to listen to this on Saturday nights in Boston, then in New Haven, and now in Brooklyn.

7:45 pm: " . . . with up-to-the-minute war news. We now return to WOR regular programming in progress."

It's such an ancient pitch

But one that I wouldn't switch . . .

Next they play "The Best is Yet to Come." I'm reading Marianne Moore's poem "The Sycamore" and as Sinatra sings the word "embrace," I read her phrase "pied at the base."

Andrew had a job interview for a teaching position at Long Island Community College. He said the chairman's office was filled with an unbelievable number of plants. "He was interviewing me and he had leaves all over his sweater!"

February 4, 1991

He didn't get the job. And I'm afraid that, once again, he'll lose the one he has.

I'm paying his grad school loans, the rent on the studio, waiting, waiting, waiting.

His disappointment, always masked. It looks and sounds like arrogance but—when you sleep with a man you understand what's under the surface. Not that he could ever be honest with me or with himself about this. To be so close to each other and to have this wall, these delusions, between us and what we could become if we worked together, if we were realistic—

Hodge's success, his false modesty, and the pleasure he takes in succeeding where Andrew (the tall, arrogant, hapless guy with the beautiful deep voice and the frustrated, formerly adoring wife) always fails—

March 12, 1991

> *American soldiers are now cleaning the hippos' pens.*
> DEBORAH WONG,
> *Kuwait City, NPR news*

One day, four different skies: lacey / prophetic / complacent / blue.

Eavesdropping with my eyes in the subway. I should make up a new word—I don't tuck myself under the eaves to listen, I ride the trains and read over peoples' shoulders, and watch, and sometimes I overhear. So what is this? Collecting? Spiritual greed?

The woman on the train reading the Psalms, her Bible wrapped in brown paper. *Señor, mi protector, a ti clamo.*

I cling to you, Lord—
Rumbling into the darkness—

August 11, 1991

From the back windows I can see my Neapolitan neighbor's garden, his
trellis, his grape arbor; after a hard rain he comes out the back door of
his basement as out of a cave and touches the wet tendrils and smashed
blossoms with infinite tenderness. Then he kicks that tomcat from the deli
when he finds him under the tarp. The man yells, the cat screams, and other
things rustle through the underbrush. And in a minute all is quiet again.

He starts to build his compost heap at the end of winter. I watch him
as I sit at my kitchen table, drinking my tea and looking down at his gar-
den from the third floor. After Easter he crowned the compost heap with
wilting lilies. One Sunday night I saw him lay nine slices of white bread
(which *glowed*) around the top of the pile, so slowly and deliberately, it
was sacramental.

In the spring when he comes out to plant, he looks up at me and
speaks to me, again, in Italian. Another winter has passed. I am still mar-
ried, still working for the same publisher, still don't have a child, and still
haven't learned Italian. I shake my head: no, I can't speak Italian; and nod:
yes, you're right, *vergogna*, it's a shame, since I am Sicilian, or half Sicil-
ian, and I look Sicilian, and I should know how to speak with you about
your garden.

Italian was the language of secrets in our house. I know only a few
words in Italian: *puzzo, vergogna, piazza* . . . stink, shame, porch. And *la
gelosia di malattia*—the sickness, jealousy. Nonnie says that in a singsong
voice.

She wasn't very playful, ever, and now she's even quieter. Lena, Joey,
Anna have all died—she's outliving her children and grandchildren. She
doesn't get to Mass very often. She watches Mass for shut-ins on TV most
Sunday mornings—sits on the couch and murmurs the prayers.

Andrew speaks Italian. He learned it when he lived in Rome for a year,
when his father was at the American Academy. He and Nonie talk to each

other in Italian. She calls him *Andrea*. He says that she's speaking Sicilian dialect—it's not really Italian. It's harsh. He likes my grandmother as much as he dislikes my mother.

"Your mother hates women," he tells me.

"But she's a woman and I'm a woman—"

"Ergo . . ."

August 16, 1991

We came home from the movies the other night to find Mr. Goldberg and his girlfriend Margaret sitting on chairs on the sidewalk in front of the building. It was too hot to stay inside. The wiring is ancient and can't support air conditioners. Mr. Goldberg was born in the building. I guess he is about seventy, but the building dates from the late nineteenth century. From the roof, where we go when it's hot, we can see the World Trade Center, the harbor, everything. Fireworks, sometimes. Glowing cigarettes down below, and shadowy back steps and silhouettes. The old man sitting in the dark in his garden, listening to the crickets, and the sirens in the distance.

October 6, 1991

In Leonardo's pocket notebooks, a paragraph of gestural descriptions:

"One who is drinking has left his glass in its position and turned his head toward the speaker. Another twists the fingers of his hands together and turns with a frown . . ."

According to Clark, these are the as-yet "unallotted" gestures of the Last Supper.

November 8, 1991

Stopped at Lamston's to buy witch hazel and Noxema. The place was undergoing reconstruction, and there was a lot of confusion at the registers, just two clerks and long lines of customers, several of them senile or mentally ill. Someone—it seemed to be one of the better dressed, sane people—smelled bad, and customers, noticing this each in her own time, jockeyed from line to line to avoid the stench.

One cashier: older woman with name tag that said "Laura." She was wearing a brutally ugly wig, like a piece of coal-colored polyester carpet treated with a curling iron. On her register, a sign: "Please pardon our appearance."

When it was my turn at the register, the other cashier, a young woman named "Mon-cherie," rang me up.

December 1, 1991

"Imagine someone pointing to a spot in the iris in a face by Rembrandt and saying, 'the wall in my room should be this color.'"

Today I went back to where I left off in Wittgenstein's *Remarks on Color* when my mother called yesterday. The laundry basket was close at hand and I had marked my place with a pair of rumpled underpants.

December 5, 1991

Dive into the mistake, so when you climb out, you're slick with it.

Reading Nabokov's *Speak, Memory*, I arrive at "the buttered verandah." But, no, that's not it; it's "the lighted verandah."

December 22, 1991

I ran into Margaret this morning. She came from Boro Park to visit Mr. Goldberg and have him take her to the doctor. She has problems with her legs. Where Mr. Goldberg is wiry, Margaret is all flesh.

I wonder how old she is? She dyes her short hair black. Retired from the post office years ago. Never married, no children. She is Italian and Catholic, and Mr. Goldberg is Jewish. I can see where the mezuzahs were fixed to the doors in the apartment when his mother was alive. His mother didn't want him to marry Margaret because she isn't Jewish.

But his mother died many years ago, and it seems that he and Margaret have been together for a while. Why didn't they marry after his mother died?

Today I asked her how long they'd been going out with each other. "Oh, about forty years."

December 30, 1991

This morning while it was still dark, Andrew was moving around the apartment, getting ready to leave on an overnight run to Pittsburgh for the art shipping company where he works on the trucks. When he leaned down to kiss me goodbye, I narrated a dream I was having at that minute: I was the soup in a can, trapped, realizing I was utterly dependent on someone coming along with a can opener to let me out.

1992

February 6, 1992

Ma's birthday. I called her. When I was growing up I had to be good to her because she had to suffer my father and all of us kids. Now I have to be nice to her because Joey's dead. She never lets me or anyone else forget it, either—she definitely works it and I am embarrassed for her sometimes. She and my father kicked him out of the house because he was gay! And now it's like she thinks she was married to my brother or something—or he was Jesus, which makes her the Blessed Mother. What about the other two boys, and me and my sister? We are drowning—we are nothing. It is so much easier to love someone who's gone and can't give you any backtalk.

When I go up to Boston and cater to my mother, Caroline rolls her eyes, sickened. She wasn't in New York sitting next to Joey in his hospital bed, watching Ma watch her son die. I was. And I don't think I could ever have a child after seeing that—could not bear that pain—

My mother had just come home from the A & P when I called.

"Such a nice retarded boy helped me with my bags. Sometimes I wish I had a nice retarded son, you know?"

I did know, I knew exactly what she meant. An uncritically loving child who could never leave home but could help pay the utility bills by working a little job at the A & P. Someone who would carry things for her.

February 17, 1992

Walked to Fort Greene today. Restaurant signs for "steam fish and bammy." Traces of the tropics among the brownstones. Very cold and sunny, verdigris steeples poking up against the taut blue sky, looking as if they could puncture and embroider it.

A man and a woman, leaning far out a window, looking in the same direction, laughing.

At the other end of the street, an edgy, bedraggled woman about my age, standing beneath another window waiting for someone to throw her dope down to her. She wears a tweedy, business-like coat, but she's not ready for work; it's wrapped around her like a bathrobe. Poor crackhead. The rag wrapped around her head and the state of her teeth make her look like she fell here from another era. Oh mother.

Across the street teenagers play in the schoolyard at Bishop Laughlin, but I can't catch a glimpse of them because the place is a fortress against drug dealing, a chain link fence tightly boarded up to keep the dealers out.

Last night I dreamed my cat was leashed to a blade of grass.

April 25, 1992

Cold spring day, and I experience the species love that come with walks in spring in Brooklyn Heights and makes me feel like Walt Whitman (in a good way).

Walking past the Church of the Pilgrims, once the scene of abolitionist sermons and a stop on the Underground Railroad. Now the porch is strewn with flattened boxes, bottles, a tattered magazine with a cover story about the new fertility treatments. Streaks of shit smeared on the stone floor.

Nearby I see a tall figure wrapped in a filthy salmon pink blanket, walking by a building freshly painted the same pretty color.

April 26, 1992

The boy on the subway near Pratt with the lavish scar from temple to dimple. The scar tissue isn't really tough yet. Voluptuous cleavage. I can see into him—the coral-colored flesh beneath his dark skin.

The temples—the sanctuary—his face—violated.

He winks at me at Flatbush Avenue when he gets off the train.

May 5, 1992

> The "imagination's Latin," composed of "speech, paint, and music."
> WALLACE STEVENS

May 8, 1992

My brother Richard was evicted from the flophouse on Merrimack Street near the Boston Garden where he's been living for years. The building inspector gave him ample warning: his room is a fire hazard. I picture towers of paper—newspapers, his books (including his beloved Pascal), his own writing—surrounding his bed, with a path cut through it so he can get in and out of the apartment.

My sister drove him back a few days later and watched as he yelled up at the windows, begging the manager (who hates him) to throw down a bag of his stuff—he'd been locked out with just the clothes on his back. The manager said, "What do you want, your filthy clothes or your filthy papers?" Richard said he wanted his papers. The manager tossed the plastic bag of clothes out the window, aiming at Richard's head and laughing.

"I burned your fucking papers, asshole!" Richard's whole life has been like this.

He's sleeping on the Common this month.

May 15, 1992

We walked further and further into Prospect Park, through the twilight, over the Greensward, and felt, rising up from the grass, a sudden green coolness. We lay in the grass watching the moon rise like a big dinner plate. Men playing soccer were arguing. They were African and it was hard to see their faces in the dark, but the ball glowed in the moonlight, and they settled their argument and went back to running and kicking.

As it got dark we left the park and walked in the beautifully laid out streets and came upon a film shoot for Martin Scorcese's *The Age of Innocence*. Artificial snow and elegant brownstones, and all of us waiting for Michelle Pfeiffer to make an appearance. One of the tech guys told us that we wouldn't notice her, she doesn't stand out from the rest. And we didn't. But a school bus filled with black teenage boys turned the corner, and as soon as they saw her, they yelled out the windows, "Yo yo yo! Cat Woman!" And she looked up at them and smiled.

May 18, 1992

In Bryant Park, an old man with thick eyebrows reading the business section of the *Times*, tears in his eyes.

May 28, 1992

In an old notebook I found an account of the rainy week we spent house sitting for C and B in Berkeley. He is the older man, French. She is his third wife, a cheery, big-boned American.

On the headboard behind their bed, a jar of Vaseline. I didn't know what it was for, but Andrew did. Next to the Vaseline, on B's side of the bed, a volume of letters from Calamity Jane to her daughter, translated into French.

Somehow, that rainy week in February, Joey tracked me down where I was staying and called me there. He was livid about everything and nothing, incoherent with rage and complaint.

Now I know that he was calling me right after he'd gone to the doctor and learned that the fungus on his tongue was the first symptom of AIDS. But he didn't say that, he just went on and on about our bitchy sister: "Someone should slap her!" I agreed, but I didn't say that. Instead, I lectured him: "She's a single mother, she's trying so hard, put yourself in her shoes."

She's the one who forced him out of the closet the summer after his senior year of high school. She snooped around and found some love letters one of his teachers had sent him—a Yale graduate, a teacher not much older than my brother was. With malice masked with concern, she showed them to our parents, who threw him out of the house. I don't know where he went. That summer I was living down the Cape, working two jobs and having fun. He never spent another night in that house again.

May 30, 1992

Reading Robert Lowell's memoir of his Boston Brahmin childhood, *91 Revere Street*. His mother's comment on their Beacon Hill address: "We are barely perched on the outer rim of the hub of decency." Those fine distinctions!

And their ranking of the Italians in Boston then: "grade A" and "grade B" Wops, "grade B" applying to Sicilians (my mother and her parents, who came from Salemi, near Trapani). There were no grade C Italians. You'd be black if you were a grade C Italian; another thing altogether.

We ourselves ranked the Irish, lace-curtain and shanty Irish.

My shanty Irish father looked down on my grade-B Wop mother.

My friend's lace-curtain Irish father calls her Syrian Christian mother a "sand nigger."

I think Andrew is exotic because he is a WASP, with educated, affluent parents and (purportedly) Mayflower ancestors, while I am from the working class. His father roomed with Kevin White at Williams College! Kevin White, the mayor! I had never even heard of Williams College when I met Andrew and his father. A gulf between us, our worlds—but to others we are just two white people.

Once, standing in Riverside Park in 1984, when I dared to worry out loud, Joseph told me he wouldn't get AIDS because he only associated with Ivy League people, not those low-life no-account sorts.

And on and on.

The narcissism of minor differences (Freud's phrase).

June 5, 1992

Two legal secretaries on the F train, carrying papers and envelopes with the firm's name. Talking about work. One gets off at 14th Street, the other smiles brightly at her as she leaves. The doors close, we move toward Brooklyn, and she keeps smiling at no one and nothing. I watch her smile fade.

June 12, 1992

I went to the studio with Andrew and read, and watched him paint. My back hurt and I was bleeding so much I thought I'd pass out if I didn't rest. He pounded his fists on the small of my back. That helps, and we always end up laughing when I'm on my hands and knees and he's hammering away at me.

The phone rings and these days it's always someone asking for Hodge Park. It is currently extremely cool to be anything but white in the art world. I half expect him to start using Ho-jun, the Korean name his parents gave him.

He came in late in the day and we gave him his messages. He returned all the calls and took careful notes as he talked. Then he got out the scotch and gave me a tumbler of that with two aspirin. He told me once that Lisa doesn't menstruate—she was anorexic when she was younger and has never really had her period regularly. How much cleaner and more elegant that would be—to remain a girl in some ways.

I fell asleep on the couch in his studio when he and Andrew started talking about the NBA draft.

Rabbit-skin glue boiling in the hot pot—Damar varnish drying—the comforting sounds of the two of them talking about basketball and washing their paintbrushes in the dirty sink.

July 6, 1992

Gertrude Stein:

There are two ways to write: One way is to write as you write, the other way is to write the way you are going to write.

And now everybody has a gift for making one sound follow another even when they hesitate.

If they really hesitate then as one word does not follow another there is no such result [beauty].

You do understand about hesitating, there is a waltz called "Hesitation" . . .

1993

January 5, 1993

Heard just now from the window that opens onto Berry Street:

"So I said, just throw the fucking omelet on the floor and shit on it, just micturate on it."

I look out the window.

The man in the leather jacket shouts obscenities, while his sweetheart clutches his arm and looks at him adoringly, encouraging him: "Yes, yes, go on . . ."

January 8, 1993

> *When the imagination is continually led to the brink of vice by a system*
> *of terror and denunciations, people fling themselves over the precipice*
> *from a mere dread of falling.*
>
> WILLIAM HAZLITT

I suppose he was talking about political systems. Bathetic to say: my family was like that. Oblivion looked good to us.

After he is beaten, which happens often, Traddles, a character in *David Copperfield*, has a habit of "bursting out" with furious, compulsive, delighted drawings of skeletons.

> *She sat down in her old place, across from the publisher, and said,*
> *'What I can't bear in this house is the way I have to turn corners to go*
> *from one room to another; always at right angles, and always to the left.*
> *I don't know why it puts me in such a bad humor. It really torments me.'*
> *The publisher said, 'Write about it, Marianne. One of these days you*
> *won't be with us anymore if you don't.'*
>
> PETER HANDKE
The Left-Handed Woman

February 7, 1993

Richard was arrested for trying to break into the Saltonstall Building in Boston. He has been living in an open shipping container in a parking lot near Northeastern, and begging in front of the Saltonstall. A woman named Beverly gave him some money and he became obsessed with her and tried to break into the building on a Saturday, when all the offices were closed. The police took him to the station and now he's in Bridgewater State Prison for the Criminally Insane.

February 8, 1993

My mother called and said I have to come home to help. I can't. I just can't. This can't be my tragedy. Let them be parents for a change.

They engineered this ongoing disaster with their negligence and cruelty. Their ignorance. They are each the youngest in the families in which they grew up—big families—they're the runts of the litter—they each resent and depend on their big sister—and their oldest child—me.

I'm resigning as the oldest. They want me to help them with another crisis? My father was impatient for Joseph to die—it took ten days—by day seven my father was tapping his foot, wondering how long this would go on, distracted by the World Series. I saw this with my own eyes. When the doctor asked me to talk to my parents about pulling the plug of the respirator, since my brother was brain-dead, I wondered if my father would race to the wall to get it over with. My parents are pro-life—

And they don't know where Richard's craziness comes from—they blame each other for it. My mother suspects it comes from my father's unknown birth mother and whoever his father was—she calls my father a bastard, and he is, literally—but all they have to do is look at themselves—they drove Richard crazy. He was the family scapegoat. And I was the police—trying to keep the other kids in line. I'm implicated in all of this, I'm part of their team, even though I'm only six years older than the youngest of the five of us. I don't believe I can be a good person unless I am a good daughter, and—my parents are crazy.

I won't go up there. I am afraid that if I go up there I will kill one or both of my parents.

I am shaking.

I am crazy, too. My mother told me I would have a terrible life if I defied her—but I have to defy her if I want to live. I am going to see a psychiatrist recommended by Wendy's brother. I don't believe in therapy, but I have to do something.

February 13, 1993

My father's birthday. My brother Michael called me, drunk and sobbing: "I'm doomed, Linda. I'm doomed. Look what happened to the other two. I'm doomed, I'm next."

February 20, 1993

Dr. W's office is on an upper floor in an NYU building near Washington Square. It's overheated and filled with tropical plants that hang over him and filter the strong afternoon sun. He gets sleepy when I talk. I think I am boring him to death. I don't know how to do this. I talked a lot the first two visits and when I stop talking, he says nothing. It is painfully awkward. I apologized for hogging the conversation. He laughed. I was serious. I am too serious.

February 24, 1993

> *A tree, for example, struck by lightning was something more than merely beautiful or sublime—it was 'picturesque.' This word in its own way has been struck by lightning over the centuries. Words, like trees, can suddenly be deformed or wrecked.*
>
> ROBERT SMITHSON,
> *in an essay on Frederick Law Olmsted*

February 26, 1993

We met for a late lunch at Odeon, had the pears in wine for dessert, then went to the movies at the Angelika. As soon as we left the theater, we knew something was wrong. There wasn't enough light, and something ominous, like an eclipse, made us look downtown. The towers of the World Trade Center were completely dark, the lights in the windows that are always on were off, and it made the twilight much darker, less benign.

Someone tried to destroy the building with a truck bomb in the basement. The futility and pathos of that attempt.

March 1, 1993

I looked up "cunt" in the dictionary. It isn't listed, and it's not listed in the OED addendum, either. But they do list "cruller."

"A 'lady'—some words have a long, thin neck that you'd like to strangle." —Jean Rhys

March 6, 1993

On the G train, someone's key ring chirps.
It must be spring.

March 7, 1993

From my apartment I can hear the band at Teddy's, and the sound of the kitchen help in the back, banging plates against the garbage can, trying to loosen the last bit of pizza, bacon, Buffalo wings.

March 15, 1993

Richard is in the Lindemann Center, getting medication after being diagnosed with schizophrenia. After a while they will send him to a halfway house in East Boston. "Only the desperate go to East Boston"—John Wieners

I told Dr. W about Richard, Caroline, Joseph, Michael, Ma, and Dad. I spend more time talking about my brothers and sister than I spend talking about myself. I don't know where I end and they begin. I can't be alright until they are alright and they will never be alright.

He was as usual very sleepy. His lids drooped as I talked, and the radiator hissed the whole time I was in there. It's very hot in his office.

I mentioned an erotically tense situation last week—Andrew and I were at Hodge's apartment, resting on Hodge's bed, watching the Knicks game, and I fell asleep and Hodge moved closer to me and stroked my head. Andrew didn't notice, or if he did notice, he didn't care. I sometimes think he is handing me over to Hodge as some kind of gift.

Dr. W woke up when I said this. He leaned forward and smiled and said, "So you like basketball?"

At last I had his attention—

March 20, 1993

In the subway, very young parents, children themselves, with their baby, the child in a stiff snowsuit, asleep in the stroller. The parents arrange and rearrange his limbs as he sleeps, fix his mittens, place his feet side by side on the stroller's footrest. They stare at him. His fat, slack cheeks vibrate slightly with the rhythm of the train on the tracks. The father adjusts the baby's feet, crosses his ankles, and sits back, satisfied, nodding at the mother.

At the counter of the Oyster Bar, I brush a roach from the palisades of my coffee cup and it scurries toward my sandwich.

The man next to me groans with pleasure as he tastes his she-crab soup.

Antony to Cleopatra: "Tonight we will walk the streets and note the qualities of people."

May 2, 1993

Steve and Nancy were in town and came to visit. We watched with great amusement and affection as Steve kept trying to position himself so he could gaze at the painting he made and gave to us last year. He could not keep his attention on the conversation, it was like he was gawking at a beautiful woman and trying hard to hide his voyeurism. It really is a beautiful painting, so subtle. Sublime, I'd say, but maybe that's an insult these days?

The guys grumbled about the plight of young white men in the art world today—there's no place for them now. If there's any painter who's even whiter than Andrew, it's Steve. He's kind of pasty, with bad skin, and his eyes are a milky blue, and his hair is really no color at all. He's from Iowa, where he saved money to go to grad school at Yale by working as an illustrator for *Hog Update*. He once showed us a cover illustration that he painted for the magazine—a picture of a hog's face—an oil portrait, really—soulful eyes—awaiting slaughter—nothing ironic about it.

April 15, 1993

Physicians used to make incisions in the heads of patients and then palm a rock, pretending it had been removed from the brain, a psychosomatic cure.

When they knew their deaths were at hand, patients might ask for gold leaf injections.

Many prints of Jesus disappeared in the course of daily use. His image was printed small on linen and the linen was then used to bandage wounds, and tiny squares of linen printed with images of Jesus on the cross were swallowed by sick men and women, or fed to dying cows.

(I wonder if these sanctified linens were ever used as menstrual rags?)

June 14, 1993

Horrible fight with Andrew.

We spoke on the phone at the end of the day, as I was getting ready to leave the office. I asked him what he wanted for dinner. I love cooking for him. He said he wanted one of my omelets, with French bread and avocado. So I asked him to pick up the fixings at the grocery store, and to get me some fruit, since I am trying to eat only fruit for breakfast these days. I knew he had enough money, because I'd given him a twenty that morning.

I got home first and he arrived soon after with eggs, avocado, bread, cheese, and no fruit. I said, "But I asked you to get me some fruit—and you only bring the things you want me to cook for you? And I'm paying for your health insurance and your student loans and you can't buy me some fruit?'

He made excuses, said the fruit at the store didn't look so good. I lost it—I cried and raged and threw a saltshaker against the wall, and locked myself in the bathroom. When I came out, he was cleaning the salt and I was so sorry and ashamed. I kneeled next to him on the floor, crying as I tried to get the salt out of the floorboards.

The next day I went to see Dr. W and told him about this fight. I was feeling especially womanly and beautiful that day—perversely so, since I had been so ugly the night before—and it was warm and I was wearing a nice dress, and men had been commenting on my beauty on the street and in the subway—and I was conscious of this as I cried and told the doctor about the omelet and the fruit and the fight.

When I finished talking, he leaned forward and said, "Don't you see? Don't you see?"

I shook my head. I didn't see.

He seemed frustrated with my slowness. "You see, you want the fruit! You want the fruit! You want your husband to give you fruit!"

I waited.

"You are a woman, you want a child, the fruit, a *baby*. You are *tired* of waiting."

I started crying, but inside I was thinking: that's kind of hokey.

June 29, 1993

For Andrew:

Painter Painting

> *Pitiless verse? A few words tuned*
> *And tuned and tuned and tuned.*
> WALLACE STEVENS

The ellipse of your heart collapses
at the ache of tangent strings pulled taut
toward scattered centers of magenta,
the numbered box of love, the weedy thing

that used to creep, that used to sing
a maudlin song, and throw a shadow on
legitimate grass, legitimate foreground,
legitimate career: the grass pressed flat
where the fox used to lay, a fox from another picture.

Then a bell rings; a log rolls; ten bells ring
inside ten latticed whitewashed cribs
and you are not afraid: the numbered box
goes where the fox once was.

August 28, 1993

Vacation in California. We stayed in a wonderfully strange town, Rodeo, out near the oil refineries. Our painter friends have huge studio spaces there, because the air is toxic so the rent is cheap. Irene and Craig have a house right near the train tracks, with a beautiful garden and a view of San Pablo Bay.

We drove up the coast to see Andrew's parents at Sea Ranch. In a hardware store in Sonoma I saw a gardening manual called *Landscaping for Privacy* and I laughed—Andrew laughed, too, but the Californians didn't understand what we found so funny. Everything's about lifestyle here—ways to make a good thing better and better—whereas in New York it's all about survival—competition and survival.

Reading Melville on a rock, looking out at the Pacific: *Billows are my foster-brothers—sorrow's technicals—infinite Pacifics—*

Reading Emerson under an apricot tree: *Every book is a quotation, and every house is a quotation out of all forests and mines and stone quarries, and every man is a quotation from all his ancestors.*

August 30, 1993

California

Lyrics & burden for freight train, harmonica, & peacock

The mind catapults a poem into the future
Girls pulse with the urge to deliver
Yarrow and oleander line the roads of the state
The crushed contraltos move back east

Here's a creamy transparency, a filmy depth
The boxcars make a nice apocalyptic sound
What does it mean when peacocks scream?
Who told you that you were naked?

Upholstery cracks in the noonday sun
Too soon new lipstick tastes of attic
A louvered cattle car rumbles to slaughter
A box of meat, a box of metaphysics

This day like others is entirely fugacious
Men die making gasoline for yachts and trucks
Blood and starch go together on a plate
The freight train slices the fat pink distance

September 1, 1993

Back in Brooklyn, sitting on my fire escape and looking down into the backyards and the vegetable gardens, reading books about gardening.

September 8, 1993

We had another horrific fight on the way to visit Kelly and Mark at the Webers' house in Bethany, where we slept in the bed where Jackie O slept when she visited Nick and Kathy. Is this even *possible*? My life is weird. What am I doing here? With him? With them? Doesn't add up. I'm damaged goods. Crazy. And they're spoiled brats.

Oh my God, I sound like my sister. I *am* my sister. I have "bettered myself" so now I get to go to parties where everyone but me has a Yale degree; and almost none of them have ever paid their own way anywhere, much less had a mother who worked as a deodorant tester at Gillette or aunts who were house cleaners. My sister laughs at my earnest attempts at self-improvement. We sit at Ma's kitchen table when I go back home— Caroline actually cackles at me, blowing cigarette smoke in my face—and I can see why.

When we got back to Brooklyn, I wrote about the fight and gave the poem to Susan. A week later she told me she had a big argument with Phillip and immediately went to her desk, slammed the door, and sat down to write. Her conclusion: "It's fun to work with rancor!"

I'm not that postmodern—I'm too sincere—I don't know if it's so fun for me—

Tossed Book of Exemplary Sonnets, Brooklyn-Queens Expressway

> *Surely — But I am very far off from that,*
> *From surely. From indeed. From the decent arrow*
> *That was my clean naiveté and my faith.*
> *This morning men deliver wounds and death.*
> *They will deliver wounds and death tomorrow.*
>
> GWENDOLYN BROOKS

He said he guessed he had his walking papers and I said,
"What?" and stared back hard, but it was up to me to figure
hermeneutics, loans and gifts, and years of disappointments
hard to name. So I just shuddered and said, "You're not very

interesting," and faced the wall next to the bed. After a while he laughed and rolled me over, and I laughed, too, thinking of the woman in the Bible—thinking, thinking, thinking—"She goes down wonderfully."

That night I wandered until I walked it off, and stopped to look at books. I bought some sample sonnets and came home happy, though it was just a cheap edition, and the printing was faint, and several pages fell out of the binding and drifted to the floor as I read it at the kitchen counter drinking a glass of milk.

But then in summer, stuck in traffic on the Brooklyn-Queens Expressway, we bickered, fought, counter-complained. Under a bridge where Hasids strolled through the heat in wigs and hats, I tossed the book of sonnets out the window, and missed it bitterly, profoundly, right away, missed all the things I ever threw away, and felt such pangs of shame, such sharp remorse, I covered my face, but not before I saw a boy on the bridge laughing at those uncaged sonnets as they flew, gladly and fast and far from us, free, over the jam-packed B.Q.E.

December 27, 1993

Nighttime. Frigid cold. Christmas lights blinking in the windows. Beethoven's late quartets lugging something up the steps.

Out on the street, a roly-poly woman hurrying home in her tight brown parka and hat, trussed like a roast.

December 30, 1993

First snowfall. Bright sunshine, around ten degrees Fahrenheit. Perfect mounds of snow on banisters. Scrape of shovels on pavement. Outside the bodega, old men sit under awnings behind bead curtains of snow dripping from the eaves as the sun heats up the roofs.

1994

January 19, 1994

Two degrees below zero when I woke up this morning, according to the radio. Andrew was going out for milk at Joe's Busy Corner. He tried to get me up from under the covers so I could make the coffee. When I burrowed under the blankets he made me laugh, in his Cat-in-the-Hat winter hat, by singing a tuneless kind of nonsense song, a ballad about my futile attempts to avoid getting dressed for work, going down into the subway, keeping my appointments.

January 30, 1994

This week we went with Stanley and Susan to see *Schindler's List*, at their invitation. The day was warm for January, but by the time we got to their house in Forest Hills, the sky had darkened. We hit a dog on the drive from Brooklyn to Queens. I didn't see it, but I heard it yelp as it glanced off the fender.

When we came out of the movie, the streets were white and hushed with snow (this really is the only way to say it!), and Stanley and Susan took us to a diner where they spoke Polish with the waitress, and then told us that they had invited us to the movie because it was the anniversary of their liberation from Auschwitz. The Russians had come to liberate them.

They bickered about the date. She said it was actually on the 15th or 16th, he said the 16th or 17th. The liberation was accidental, they said. The Russians were on their way to somewhere else, and the Germans knew they were coming and fled the camp. So when Stanley and Susan (then called Stasha and Zosha) woke up, they were free. But they had nowhere to go, so stayed there for three days.

It sounds like a tale from the Brothers Grimm, the way they tell it. Horrific fairy tale. How did they survive? I have a hundred questions, but it didn't seem right to ask.

We talked about the movie. All of their refugee friends had already seen it, but they waited for us. (Susan's sister in Israel had not seen it, and wondered why Susan should: "What are you, a masochist?")

Stanley was angry after the movie, spouting off about the Nazis, but it was more comic or pathetic than tragic to witness his bluster. Susan was uncomfortable, as if he were exaggerating or just being a bit uncouth (she is much more glamorous and refined in her manner than he is; pathos and melodrama make her uncomfortable). She tried to change the subject. "Did you know that Mr. Cohen [her boss at the travel agency where she works] is starting to offer tours to Romania?" We were all silent at the attempt to switch gears. If only it weren't the Holocaust, weren't History that hurt so much. If only it had been a mere insult to Stanley's masculinity, the kind of thing that makes wives roll their eyes in an everyday way.

The kasha came to the table, and then the cutlets and the sauerkraut. We ate and told dirty jokes, and soon we were screeching with laughter (except for Susan, who just smiled). Stanley told a few WASP jokes, grinning slyly at Andrew. "Why don't WASPs have roaches? Because they never have any food in the house!"

But then with coffee we went back to talking about the movie.

"Wasn't Ben Kingsley great?" said Stanley.

We agreed. Kingsley had played Schindler's right-hand man, a Jew in a moral and historical vise.

"And he's not even Jewish," Stanley said. "Amazing!"

"Are you sure he's not Jewish?" I asked.

Stanley looked at me as if I were out of my mind.

"No, he's not Jewish! How could he be Jewish? He's Gandhi! He was Gandhi! Didn't you see Gandhi? He's not Jewish! He's a Hindu!"

Susan stood, elegant as ever but a little shaky with vertigo. She pulled her sweater snugly over her hips and checked to see if her clip-on earrings were in place. She arranged herself with back and shoulders toward Stanley, waiting for him to help her with her fur coat.

We went out into the street, where the snow was very heavy and the changing traffic lights were doing wonderful things to it.

We dropped them off at their house and as we drove away, Stanley called out, "Be careful, you have a Jew in your car." (He knows that there is supposed to be a Jewish grandfather somewhere in my family, but still I was surprised, and laughed.)

But later we realized that he had said to Andrew, "Be careful, you have a jewel in your car."

It would not occur to me or to Andrew to think of me as a precious gem.

February 4, 1994

Nina Berberova:

> *We will speak of awareness. No suffering is too high a price to pay for awareness. Millions of innocents will be resurrected if consciousness awakens . . . their sufferings were terrible, but will be much more terrible if they do not lead to knowledge.*

I would like to see the Russian cemetery in Paris, Sainte Genevieve-les-Bois.

In her memoir Berberova seems to grow younger as she ages. She goes to America and talks about separating herself from the other Russians who insulated themselves from all things American: "All this pedestrian tribal dust, brought along, was being spread within and around themselves."

February 27, 1994

I am about seven weeks pregnant. I can't believe it. I was distracted by a horrible flu last month, and then, for a long time, I thought I was just having extraordinary PMS. It wasn't an accident (Andrew promised me years ago that "some day" we'd have a baby—and now his friends have babies—so he thought we should do it). Still, I'm surprised. It was easy and it happened so fast, after all these years of not making babies.

I can't give up coffee completely. I'm drinking half decaf as I sit on the Brooklyn Promenade, all bundled up. I look over at the buildings of lower Manhattan. I never tire of sitting here and looking over at the harbor, the boats, the sky, the buildings. How can all those heavy buildings sit on the edge of that wafer of land?

March 1, 1994

We went to an orientation given by the midwives who work at St. Vincent's Hospital. I have a high threshold for pain and I mentioned this to the midwives and they just laughed. Of course I don't know what the pain of childbirth will be like. They're the experts.

Today on the Brooklyn Bridge someone shot at a van filled with Hasidic students, wounding four, two very badly. It is said that the attacker was Arab and that this was retaliation for the murders in the mosque in Hebron last Friday.

The victims are in the ICU at St. Vincent's, and tonight we passed through tight security to get into the maternity ward for orientation. The lobby was filled with policemen, hospital public relations people, reporters, and young Hasidic men. As we left the hospital, boys were nodding and praying at the 12th Street wall of St. Vincent's while a TV crew washed them in bright lights and filmed them.

We saw newborns in the nursery before we left. Infants who will grow up to kill or be killed? Each sleeping tonight in a pastel cap.

April 13, 1994

Andrew at the kitchen table, reading his book and drinking his morning tea. I was in bed and he brought me my coffee and read me some ribald sections of Aristophanes' "The Birds." Fanning himself like an old maid when he got to the raunchiest bits, and flapping his house slippers, too.

April 19, 1994

Even as a child I knew I had to leave Boston to come to New York. To paraphrase Wallace Stevens, people were not going to dream of baboons and periwinkles there, so I had to come here.

My baby will be a New Yorker.

May 6, 1994

For my birthday, since I can't drink wine now, I indulged in sweets. I went down to Economy Candy and bought Necco wafers. Pure nostalgia, and they're not even my favorite, but the smell reminds me of the air around MIT, near the Charles River and the Dudley bus stop, when the Necco factory was baking wafers—spearmint atmosphere, wintergreen sunsets, candy-flavored rain.

Economy Candy—"What a euphonious appellation," as W. C. Fields would say. We watched "My Little Chickadee" last night. It's great when he paws at Mae West's hotel room door and says, in that insinuating voice, "I have some pear-shaped ideas to discuss with you."

I feel like a pear-shaped idea myself.

May 10, 1994

I've lost my cover. I used to go out in an oversized men's gabardine shirt and baggy pants and chunky shoes, with my short hair, so as to observe rather than be the object of attention. I learned that my femininity on the street made it hard for me to look and listen. So I toned it down.

But now that I am pregnant, I am the spectacle. In Union Square and in Bryant Park, the men on the benches comment as I pass. Sometimes the commentators are lucid, sometimes they're relatively benign, and sometimes they're crazed or overtly raunchy. (I'm not fazed, especially since my schizophrenic brother Richard tried to convince me to marry him last time I saw him; but that conversation fizzled, thank God, since he was on his way to save a stripper in Swampscott, and the cab he drives was idling in the parking lot of the funeral home. He was afraid to turn the car off—it was a bitterly cold night and the engine was ready to die—and he had to go.)

These men on the sidelines focus on the fact that I am knocked up, visibly fucked—good for me!—or: the joke's on me!—and most of them tell me that I should have a son.

May 15, 1994

Any kind of accuracy, even flattering, scares people, I suppose.
— ELIZABETH BISHOP

We've moved back to Carroll Gardens, as it can't be good to be pregnant in Williamsburg, where, at night, you can smell all the poisons coming from small factories. Our new landlady looks like Harpo Marx.

Yesterday I saw the old man with his pony cart, selling seedlings from the back of the cart. Does he have a greenhouse where he grows these things? In a few months he'll have pots of basil, or basilico, as we called it growing up among Sicilians. My grandmother grew basilico and tomatoes on her piazza on Belgrade Avenue.

At the store that sells candy, school supplies, toys, lottery tickets, and light bulbs, two handmade signs, one announcing that someone has found an elderly Chihuahua, another advertising slush puppies.

At a bakery on Court Street, a big, humid-looking print of the meaty Sacred Heart of Jesus, and below it, another sign: "Take a number."

May 24, 1994

I felt the baby move for the first time a few weeks ago. I was sitting in a rocking chair near my desk and my pelvis was tipped back. I felt like an aquarium.

They call this "quickening."

Who is this I'm carrying?

"Be not forgetful to entertain strangers; for thereby some have entertained angels unawares."—Hebrews, 13:2

May 28, 1994

On Sunday we went to the Met to see the Petrus Christus show. Small and not crowded. My favorite painting was the Annunciation, which is in the permanent collection, but I'd never looked at it before. I liked the way the angel's wings hovered over a fork in the road that made the roads look like echoes of the figure.

Then we walked up the avenue, happening past Jackie Onassis's apartment building, where throngs of people waited for someone famous to come out from the post-funeral gathering. I saw Pat Lawford in a pink suit, but everyone else looked past her, waiting for John-John or Caroline, I guess.

A sunny, brilliant, perfect day. We could smell water all the way up the FDR drive as we drove along the East River—Gerard Manley Hopkins "wild air, world-mothering air,"

> *dear*
> *Mother, my atmosphere*
> From *"The Blessed Virgin*
> *Compared to the Air We Breathe"*

June 3, 1994

> *The "ever jubilant weather" is not a symbol. We are physical beings in a physical world; the weather is one of the things that we enjoy, one of the unphilosophical realities. The state of the weather soon becomes a state of mind. There are many "immediate" things in the world that we enjoy; a perfectly realized poem ought to be one of these things. This last remark, by-the-way, has nothing to do with "Waving Adieu". People ought to like poetry the way a child likes snow & they would if poets wrote it.*
>
> WALLACE STEVENS *in a letter to*
> *Hi Simons, January 9, 1940*

June 7, 1994

I lost my wedding ring in the subway. I was rushing to get the F train at Fifth Avenue—it was so hot, I couldn't stand the thought of waiting on the grubby subway platform in the heat—and as I ran, I twiddled my ring with my thumb as I sometimes do when I'm anxious or busy. And so I watched it fly off my finger and onto the tracks just as the train left the station.

One other person had just missed the train, and he saw what happened to my ring. The look on his face as he took it all in—my big belly, my lost wedding ring, my distress. Now he was distressed, too. He was an Orthodox Jew and he hesitated to approach me, but after a minute he stepped toward me and gestured, volunteering to go down onto the tracks to retrieve my ring, which we could both see clearly. I laughed and said, "No, thank you so much, please don't do that." I was imagining the cover story in the *Daily News* the next day—"Jewish Father of Ten Dies Trying to Rescue Cheap Wedding Band for Pregnant Woman."

My wedding ring cost nine dollars in 1986. I thought it didn't matter, I would just replace it. But when the next train came, I couldn't get on it. I couldn't just leave my wedding ring there. The man looked at me as he stepped onto the train and I stayed behind. I let two more trains pass and thought, "This is silly." And I went home and told Andrew about it and he laughed.

I saw it again the next day, and the next, and the third day it was gone. A crew had come to clean up all the detritus on the tracks.

June 18, 1994

Business trip to London, alone, five months pregnant. I could not convince Andrew to come with me.

I'm used to doing a lot by myself but maybe this is too much.

I had a weekend to myself before I had to start calling on magazine editors and I spent it walking. As I walked along the canal and into Camden, I turned down a road lined with tall row houses. I saw a young man stumble out a front door and down the steep front steps. He saw me, too, and waited for me, and my guard went up. He fell into step with me as I passed and began to chat. He was high, I guessed, but not murderous or insane, so I relaxed a bit. "How are you?" he asked. When I answered him, he went on alert: "Are you American?"

"Yes," I said.

"Where are you from?"

"I live in Brooklyn."

"Brooklyn. That's where that Baruch Goldstein was from, the guy who massacred Arabs in the mosque in Hebron."

This was true. It had happened a while back, and was big news in New York City. This was the first thing that came to mind when I mentioned Brooklyn? What was it to him?

"Are you Jewish?" he asked.

Time to think quickly. Yes, maybe a little, by way of my father's father. And if you are anti-Semitic, I certainly don't want to associate myself with you as a fellow gentile. And I'm so Catholic—

Oh, Linda, lighten up. This is a total stranger, a passing encounter. You can't make up for the anti-Semitism of the Vatican during WWII no matter what you say in reply to this question.

"No," I said, "I'm not Jewish."

He stopped and scrutinized my face intensely, like a surgeon accustomed to handling warm, throbbing ethnicities with his bare hands while the clock ticks.

"Irish and Sicilian?" he said.

I gasped.

"Exactly right. Wow. I'm impressed. I'm amazed. I do that kind of ethnic dissection all the time, but here you are a Londoner and I'm an American and how did you—"

He laughed and asked me if I wanted to drop some acid with him,

"No!" I said. "Haven't you noticed that I'm pregnant?"

At that he looked down at my belly and smiled with respect and awe.

We walked companionably to the corner, where we said goodbye and good luck to each other.

June 19, 1994

On Monday I went to see the editors at *New Scientist* to tell them about fall books we're publishing and, as soon as I started to speak, the baby kicked wildly. I'd been virtually silent for a day and a half, and it was as if she wondered where I'd gone.

She kicked a lot when I went to Gissing's neighborhood, Clerkenwell, and took a tour of the old prison there. A charming bearded elf of an historian gave us a tour. All the other tourists were British—parents, students, some little kids. He started talking about Irish people, and they all laughed. I didn't get the joke. He was telling us about some Irish prisoners in the nineteenth century, who took themselves to be Republicans and freedom fighters rather than common criminals, and tried to bomb their way out, and failed miserably, as you would expect Irishmen to do when dealing with fire, massive stone prison walls, and the British Empire.

At the Midtown Manhattan library, preparing for my trip to England, I'd searched for books about the Irish famine. I'd grown up hearing about the way the English starved the Irish, but it was so vague, and I wanted history. In the card catalog I found these subject headings:

Famine, Africa

Famine, Humor

Famine, Ireland

I left with half a dozen books and learned that the English were exporting Irish food while the Irish starved. Sometimes they set up enormous iron pots of India meal and the people were so desperate, they were burned by the boiling corn meal as they clamored for a taste.

Funny, funny famine.

June 20, 1994

Met with an editor from the *London Review of Books* to talk about spring titles. Nice guy. Working-class. I'm comfortable with him as I am not with most of the other people I meet in publishing, here in England or back home.

I'd met him once before, and when I made the appointment this time, I didn't mention I was pregnant. He looked alarmed when he saw me come in the door of the pub. I saw him glance at my ring finger when we sat down, and later he asked me if the father was still in the picture. "Oh," I said. "Very much so. We've been married eight years, together for longer than that." We talked then about books and class. He is writing a novel.

Later I went to the outdoor market at Covent Garden and bought myself a new wedding ring. Twenty dollars.

June 21, 1994

Walked and walked and ended up in Hyde Park. I sat in the grass and watched people gather in anticipation of a concert, and soon the brass band showed up. They practiced and they spit and they sounded great. And then they burst into a melody, familiar immediately from all the times I'd listened to it while grieving my brother's death—one of the "Chants d'Auvergne" on a Pathé album that Joey bought at a flea market. But now the music was round and brassy and droll, and so was I. I laughed out loud at the surprise—this song of longing redeemed by this happy unexpected rendition in a foreign place.

August 16, 1994

Road trip with Andrew. Maybe the last one we will take for a while. Driving along the parkways on Long Island, thinking about the master builder, Robert Moses. They say he planned the overpasses so they'd be a little too low for buses to pass under them—he didn't want to make it too easy for the masses to escape the boroughs and invade the beaches of Long Island.

Landscaping for Privacy

> *Make a pagoda of thyself!*
> HERMAN MELVILLE

> *Ultima multis!*
> INSCRIPTION ON A MEDIEVAL SUNDIAL

The hedges along the parkway the trees, the trees—
They sashay, they nearly genuflect, they breathe.
It's good to breathe; it's good to get away in summer,
it makes you feel clean. The city, the squalor, the mess,

that's what's killing us. Did I tell you about the rat
I saw in the subway last night? It had a swollen belly
and no fear, it went right for a queen in heels.
Enough, I know; not here, not now; I should relax,
shut up, let go. Oh, yes, Long Island's very fresh and nice.
Do they have rats out here or just field mice?
And I forget, what do people do with themselves
in the suburbs? The streets are empty,
the lawns unused. If I lived here, I'd spread out,
I'd hang a hammock, I'd keep sheep, I'd dig a well.
I'd build hummocks to my own specs,
I'd be positively pastoral.

You're right, of course. Of course you're right.
I couldn't keep sheep, there's probably an ordinance,
they'd shoot me for ruining property values.
But what's property, anyway? Years ago
I read about a pillar of roses in an English garden
and so I own it, I have the deed by heart.
Speaking of which, pull over, look,
here's a surprise for you. Check out my bicep.
Do you like my new tattoo?

What do you mean, "What is it, did it hurt?"
It's a miniature gazebo, of course it hurt!
Note the incredible detail, the wicked craftsmanship.
See—it's a garden pagoda for me and you,
with ivy and grass, and a snake in the grass.
Hey, what are you doing? Oh, yes, that's good,
Yes, kiss it and make it better.
Because it did hurt a bit. In fact,
it hurt like hell. (Remember that night
when you touched me and I yelled?)

Okay, let's drive, let's tour the hydrangeas
and the lawns. What could be more suggestive
than a grassy mattress? Maybe that TV glowing
in a darkened den, shades nearly drawn.
Slow down, slow down—that's strange—
a sick room, a suburban tomb, on a day like this,
with clouds all starched and bustling
in a Disney sky. Look, they have a gazebo, too,
jam-packed with rusted rakes and trash.

If I had their lawn, I'd soak it and sunbathe on it,
I'd sleep out under the stars, I'd walk to the mall
and strap a sack of fertilizer to my back
and hike all the way home. We've lived in the city
far too long, yes, that's what's killing us.
That and this monument to love, this brick
inscribed FOREVER. Let's let it sink.
Let's kiss. I'll take the wheel, I'll drive
so you can look at clouds.

"All clouds are clocks," bulldozing time.
Do you remember who said that?
A pauper? A philosopher?
Well, he was right.
Those clouds are bullies,
white armadas, pretty and cruel,
ushering last days for many.

September 8, 1994

In the main reading room of the New York Public Library at lunch today,
the quiet madman with the enormous book under his threadbare shirt.
Conspicuously outlined under the fabric, like a shield or a bullet-proof
vest. His secret.

And me with my huge belly.

I think of searching for my father's mother, the Irish woman lost to us. To shame.

Unmarried, poor, pregnant in 1931.

Impossible search. Makes me think of that great Irish oxymoron, Gloria Bog, in the place about which John McGahern writes. "They were coming into country they knew. They had suffered here."

Last night I dreamed that I was riding a bike at night through the Mattapan ghetto, circa 1969, on the way to Nonnie's house in Roslindale. I had a mattress tied around my waist that made it impossible to steer my bicycle and hard to see where I was going. And I was trying to read a book while riding my bike.

October 2, 1994

Another anniversary, eight years, Joseph; two days before I am due to give birth. It's like the other half of my New York parentheses: that death, this life.

She is due, or I am due, or we are due, on October 4th.

I can see the baby's heel under my left rib.

November 10, 1994

She's here, sleeping on my lap while I try to write. I'm so tired. She's so beautiful. *And I am worthy.* Andrew said that's what I said the minute I pushed her out into the world.

The midwives didn't believe me when I said I had a high threshold for pain—they laughed and said they'd know when I was fully dilated—but they didn't know, they couldn't tell, I wasn't complaining enough, they didn't hear me when I called to say it was awful and could one of them please meet me at the hospital? Barbara said there was no way I was ready—and I doubted myself when they doubted me, and I almost ended up having the baby on the floor in the kitchen.

Turns out that Barbara's shift was ending and she didn't want to meet me at the hospital and be stuck with me while I labored on for hours and hours.

I learned after it was over that I had what's called a back labor, altogether brutal, with the baby's head pressing against my spine the whole time, no relief from that pain between contractions. We were watching a video, *Six Degrees of Separation*, when the pains started. Andrew fell asleep and then things really took off. I kept squatting and counting, I took a shower, I cried, I thought about Jesus, I was out of my mind. But I was quiet. I called the midwife but apparently she mistook my quietude for a lack of serious pain, and wouldn't allow me to come to the hospital. She thought I wasn't dilated enough. What did I know?

I begged Andrew to call her and get her permission to bring me to the hospital. He did, and then he called a car service to drive us across the bridge to St. Vincent's.

In the car I squatted in the back seat. A little water trickled out of me. The driver was panicked. When he dropped me off at St. Vincent's, there was just a revolving door, and I tried to get in and through it on my knees. Two orderlies saw me and rushed out with a wheelchair. Upstairs the midwife, a skinny elegant woman who always wore leather in the office, had me kneel on my hands and knees (my back hurt so much I couldn't sit or rest on my back) and then she put a fist up my coolie. "Oh wow," she said. "You're ready. Ten centimeters! You can push." But I was too exhausted and panicked to push.

Finally I did it, I pushed. How, I don't know. And I was no longer quiet. I was sure the baby would break me, I couldn't do it, Andrew was giving me tiny sips of water while I held on to the monkey bars above me, pushing, pushing, and then there she was—and all the backed-up water that hadn't come out of me splashed in Andrew's face and the midwife's, too, as they caught the baby, and I laughed.

She was so beautiful in her father's arms. Perfect and slimy. And I was no longer in pain. But I can't forget the pain, though they say I will. I wonder if I ever will forget him holding her, and handing her to me.

It's not like she fulfills me, exactly. It's as if her existence, her coming through my body and out between my legs, authorizes me as an animal.

She cries every night for three or four hours, and sometimes I think I'm going crazy, I'm so tired. But her shit really does smell sweet.

November 14, 1994

My brother Michael is getting married to his dream girl. Lace-curtain Irish, daughter of a New York City police detective. The wedding shower is this weekend in Long Island. My mother came down for it and stayed with us in Brooklyn for three days. Great to see her holding Isabel, but exhausting to take care of both of them; my mother went tits-up on my couch and stayed there all day, every day. She is too fat to walk very far. I cooked for her, I lectured her about healthy eating, I brought her cold cloths for her forehead. She hemmed the enormous flowered dress she'd bought to wear at Eileen's shower—she's so short, nothing fits unless she hems it—and I ironed it for her.

She was embarrassed when I nursed Isabel. I said, "Didn't Nonnie breastfeed you and your sisters and Stevie?" She looked disgusted—a facial expression that comes to mind whenever I think of my mother— and made a noise like she was about to throw up. "Ach! She was an immigrant! She didn't know any better!"

Andrew and I tried to go out to dinner on Atlantic Avenue, but my mother panicked and called the restaurant because Isabel was crying and wouldn't stop. She's colicky, she cries like that with us, too. We raced home and were happy to be back with our baby.

I was changing Isabel's diaper, my mother standing next to me at the table, and Isabel was looking up at the crystal chandelier. This is new, the way she can focus on something. We marveled at her while she marveled at the sparkling light.

"Look at her," my mother said. "She's *mesmotized!*"

I laughed with delight. "Great word, Ma!"

My mother grinned up at me like a punk, proud of herself. Another look that is pure Mary Cammarata, as the Irish relatives call her. My father and all of us kids are so much taller than she, yet she dominates us. She's remorseless, a bully. But she can be *mesmotizing* at times.

I don't think she realized she'd coined an entirely new word. I will use it often, I'm sure.

November 27, 1994

Byron de la Beckwith, the killer of Medgar Evers, left his rifle behind, and the morning dew froze his fingerprint on the rifle. But still he was acquitted.

I can read that, record that, because it is historical, frozen, and the search for justice continues. But I have to stop reading the papers, now that I have a baby. That girl who was gang raped on the trash heaps off Kent Avenue, the slaughter in Rwanda. I sit here nursing this child, and see how much work it is. Endless work. My whole life goes into making a life for her, growing her in my body, giving birth, caring for her, looking at her face, cleaning her, feeding her. How can all that work and life be destroyed so easily? These rapists and killers never gave birth to a child. Or did they? There are women among the murderers in Rwanda. How can that be?

December 3, 1994

First trip to Manhattan with Isabel on the subway. Incredibly stimulating to be able to eavesdrop again. And I even read vicariously, looking over the baby's head in the snuggly and over shoulders at newspapers and romance novels. My favorite line today, from a bodice ripper: "Aye, mayhap I will."

December 15, 1994

My first trip into Manhattan without the baby. I went looking for something to wear to Michael's and Eileen's wedding. It was weird to leave Isabel, who has been either in or on me at all times for almost twelve months now. I got off the A train at the World Trade Center, since it was the closest place to shop in Manhattan, closest to the water that separated me from Isabel in Brooklyn. (What did I think I would do if I had to get back to her quickly, swim to the Brooklyn Promenade?)

Shopping in the mall under the World Trade Center is like shopping at any mall. You could be in New Jersey.

December 19, 1994

I think I'm going crazy from lack of sleep. My demons—

She won't take a bottle from anyone, nurses ten or more times a day, cries so much—the pediatrician says her stomach hurts, her gastrointestinal system has not matured yet. I can't make her happy. I feel like a cow. I can't fit into my old clothes.

It's cold now and not so easy to get outside with her and all her stuff. I miss work. But I dread going back to work and leaving her. And I have to work. I'm the worker. For the first time in his life, Andrew is working full time and not painting. But that won't last. He's not cut out for it. I was born to work.

There's something wrong with my tailbone and my right forearm— from sitting on the couch for hours and hours, holding her. Sometimes I'm paralyzed, can't seem to get her settled so I can take a shower.

Hodge stopped by with a bag of groceries yesterday. I looked awful. That doesn't matter anymore.

I cried after he left. He is judgmental about my colicky baby, he says it's because I didn't give up coffee when I was pregnant.

Their baby is so easy. The reason Andrew decided he was finally ready to have a baby: they had one.

But they don't have to go to work. He's an art world star now and his parents subsidize everything. So Hodge can stop by and bring me groceries. And criticize people who leave their babies in daycare. I have to work! What else can I do?

I am glad I never succumbed to his charms. If he'd been caught, he'd have blamed it all on me. He's even more of a blamer than I am. Two curious, seductive people with outsized superegos and perfectly suitable mates. People who want to be above reproach while playing with fire.

It's time to leave New York. This can't go on. The tension when we're all together is hard. Is it all in my head? *La malattia di gelosia.*

Anyway, it's impossible to believe I was ever beautiful enough for anyone to desire me. I am a cow now.

Andrew comforted me last night when I cried about Isabel's colic. He said that I'd secretly expected to give birth to a four-year-old child, not an infant. That's true! I love kids—but I've never been one of those women who idealized babies. And now I am ferociously in love with a tiny screaming person I can't please.

December 21, 1994

Begged Andrew to take a morning off from work to watch Isabel—there's an open sore near my tailbone and it's leaking pus. It smells awful. I don't have a doctor—my usual approach is: tough it out. But this is getting worse and worse. So I called my midwife and she recommended a guy in the Village.

It was a cold, grey depressing day. The F train sat in a tunnel under the river and for a long time I was trapped in a car with crazy man who was ripping his clothes off with a knife. I miss the old train cars. You could walk from car to car in the '80s—you could escape. Graffiti on the sides of the trains wasn't as scary as being trapped with a psycho in a tunnel.

When at last I got to the doctor's waiting room, I found an emaciated man with Kaposi's lesions sitting with his head in his hands. Another wasted guy came out of the doctor's office and this one went in. What was I doing here, post partum in my enormous, itchy, woolen pants? When it was my turn the receptionist waved me in and the doctor asked me to take off my clothes. Then he checked my tailbone and told me I had strep in my back. I never heard of such a thing. I asked what caused it. He said it could be lots of things. He looked at my fat butt and pressed the pus-filled blister: "It certainly isn't because you're malnourished." He gave me a prescription for antibiotics and sent me home, where Andrew was not disgusted by me and helped me to clean my open sore. But I raged at him anyway. Disgusted with myself.

1995

January 13, 1995

One difference between the beauty of fashion models and movie stars
and the beauty of everyone else: the camera captures the model's beauty,
even increases it; but the beauties of other people often elude the cam-
era. So you read biographies in which everyone testifies to the legendary
beauty and charisma of so-and-so, and you turn to the photo insert and
are unimpressed.

Ordinary beauty flourishes elsewhere—across card tables, in carriage
houses, at stoplights, during a frenzy of snow shoveling before turning in
for the night. During awkward goodbyes. In life.

January 20, 1995

Last night Isabel got confused and started suckling before she was
attached to the nipple; gave me a tiny hickey on the side of my breast.

The book says some women lactate at the sound of a baby's cry. This
morning a car alarm went off and my milk flowed.

February 2, 1995

The sex educator on the radio is talking about Ravel's "Bolero:" "It builds
to climax over and over again."

Ma used to play "Bolero" at top volume while vacuuming the house.
On the hi-fi, as my father called it.

She also liked to play the Tijuana Brass while doing housework.

And "Lara's Theme," from the soundtrack of *Doctor Zhivago*. (Poor
Pasternak.)

February 8, 1995

Everything is liquid today:

Claret, the fluid old-time sports writers loved to see streaming from
the noses of boxers.

T. E. Hulme's definition of romanticism: "a spilt religion."

Andrew boiling Isabel's rattles and building blocks; a toy soup.

March 1, 1995

The old woman in a spangled green knit cap and the garish makeup. She stands in a doorway next to the little market at Carroll Park.

Dreary gray day. She goes into the shop.

"What's up, Mary?" asks one of the deli men.

"What's up?" she answers. "Poverty, despair, loneliness. That's what's up."

April 5, 1995

I don't know if I dreamed it or actually found it in the O.E.D.—the word for a significant, luminous dissenter who appears in the background when the photo of a crowd scene is scrutinized closely and repeatedly. As if the photograph only developed completely upon examination.

The picture of Con Markiewitz speaking at a rally for Irish independence in County Kilkenny in 1917. The face of the lone female looming in the crowd, a moon among bullets.

April 7, 1995

The word made flesh—

So this was a chancre—
Like the Louvre—or macabre—
More like a sculpture than a sore—
A crater—a badge and not a wound—

I run my tongue around it to be sure.

The Suburbs of a Secret
A Strategist should keep

EMILY DICKINSON

April 13, 1995

The hound moans and yelps at dawn. She is giving birth to the sun, its head is crowning.

June 7, 1995

At the locked used-car lot the other day, a pit bull with a huge penis. Scary. But why so scary?

I glanced up, my mind already on other things, and saw the scrawled paint on the window of a used Grand Am: FULLY LOADED.

On the subway today, dozens of schoolchildren on a field trip, admiring Isabel—

"Que linda," they whispered, staring at her. They all wore nametags.

Good luck in life, Kenny Best, Hector Jiminez, Lilibeth Ramos.

June 10, 1995

Two teenagers with hair dyed pink zip by me on Rollerblades.

One to the other: "That guy with the lizard on his head thinks we're weird because we have pink hair."

And indeed, when I look across the street, I see another teenager, with a lizard on his head, glancing skeptically at the Rollerbladers.

June 26, 1995

At the Brooklyn Public Library:

A girl with sutures in her eyelid

Many editions of biographies of Jackie Robinson

The flasher in the stacks, his hard-on bobbing slightly as he reads an illustrated guide to breastfeeding (a book I own, but have only skimmed)

The old woman in the dirty pink turban, reading an issue of *Cosmopolitan*

"Dirty turban" excites me the way "Smyrna merchant" might have thrilled Eliot.

June 14, 1995

The fontanelle, the hollow between two muscles, the space between places—

Un-neighborhoods, the urban hollows—

A patch of hell on earth near the Brooklyn-Queens Expressway where, one brutally hot day, I saw a raving, naked man crawling up a junk heap under the scorching sun.

So close to the apartment where Marianne Moore lived with her mother, translating the fables of La Fontaine and correcting infelicities in poems of Hart Crane and Elizabeth Bishop, campaigning to save a tree in Prospect Park, and making of moral and linguistic probity a bohemian outpost in Brooklyn.

She was wild, she was civilized, she kept nickels in a bowl near the door, as a kindness to her guests, Auden and the others, and sent them on their way back to Manhattan with subway fare.

"Brooklyn," she said, "has afforded me . . . the kind of tame excitement on which I thrive."

Lyric and Burden

Box of Water

The prospect of working with Duke
had extraordinary advantages.
Billy went all out, took the subway
and wrote "A Train," just like that.
"Where did you learn to write music the way you do?"
Duke asked Strayhorn.
"Oh—in high school," Billy replied.
Which was true.

The three musicians huddled together
for about five minutes.
The sticky three, thought Billy,
as he reached for a clean ashtray.

It was only a matter of time
before someone, black or white,
recognized his talent—
"Mr. Ellington says come back
next week at the same time."

Duke didn't question Billy's masculinity,
He knew his man
("What fun if you were a classic!"
said Gerard Manley Hopkins to Robert Bridges)
and soon he called on him
with a special assignment:
Late nights on the phone,
singing Lena Horne to sleep.

B Natural

Strayhorn was definitely trying to do a classical thing with a jazzy touch.
"Bach liked to do it, Lou. Try it. You'll like it, too."

That was the day he selected the clothes his mother would be buried in.
His Satin Doll. "Now," he said, "I don't have to worry."

Johnny Mercer was brought in to replace Strayhorn's Oedipal lyrics.
Strayhorn's original lyrics to "Satin Doll" are not known to have survived.

Lena called every night: "Hello purple people. Talk to me, honey.
What are we thinking about?"

"We're thinking about flavoring milk with ashes."

Sonnet in Search of a Moor

I fell asleep reading David Hajdu's biography of Billy Strayhorn,
thinking: I must find and listen to that piece of music Strayhorn wrote
on a Shakespearean theme, the one with the beautiful title . . .

And then I dreamed that I'd camped out in the wilderness, on a moor
near the ocean. I'd brought my TV. I'd plugged it in with a long cord,
which unfurled behind me as I walked across the moor.

Under the open moonless sky, far from buildings or people, I sat and
watched cartoons, and when I got up to hike back to town as the sun
went down, I left the TV on, a box of light on a slab of rock, the only
light that night.

Blood Count

To make an impression on Ellington, Strayhorn wrote "Chelsea Bridge."
The musicians at that session were very uncomfortable faking their way
across "Chelsea Bridge."

Actually, by then he was beyond making an impression.

That was after he went to Rosemary Clooney's house to rehearse with
her because her pregnancy was difficult and she couldn't travel. He sat
at the foot of her bed as they made the recording and when they were
finished he asked her, "Did you like your part?" Like something God
might ask you at the end of your gig.

"Blood Count" he wrote at the end, when he was reduced to pouring
booze into a tube directly into his stomach under his dinner jacket.
There were roses all over the piano, very Duchess-of-Windsor. Or was
that "Chelsea Bridge"?

No. There were no roses then. When he played "Blood Count" it was
in a darkened room, and the piano was bare except for moonlight
mammographed across its surface.

Monk

"Epistrophy" ends

as church bells begin.

"If You Can Hear It, You Can Have It"

The church bells ring down by the lake under the overpass
music scalloped by the waves of traffic on 580
dignified by rhythm and inevitability

The traffic sings, but not to me:

If I can imagine kissing a man's eyelids,
I can imagine
kissing a man's eyelids . . .

Walking and thinking, like Werner Herzog,
and hearing things inside other things:
"'The fare tonight shall be fowl,'
says the innkeeper in the stillness."

Her Way

The small coral-colored sandals from Morocco,
nailed to the wall,
match the bodice of her dress—

In the picture Callas plays that sofa like a piano,
its cleavage urgent, packed—

Unbound it would be a mess of stuffing;
stitched, it's a temptation
a box knife could undo.

At a Supper Club

Tortured
torch singer

recorded live
at the Bitter Root—

that last note
a spangle or a shingle

sewn or nailed
into place

on a
bodice or
a sloping roof—

Did she suffocate
or did she fall to her death?

Did she die of burns
or heartache?

Play it again
and wonder.

Goodness and Mercy

After we gave up, you put a record on.
Django Reinhardt played hard
on the other side of the room.
You started to snore.

An hour into it
a sideman shouted
"Play it!"
and woke you up.

We laughed.
Why did he call out just then?

Was it a photoflash
that triggered it?
A woman across the room?
A flicker of a psalm?

Yea, he was playing
in the valley of death
in a smoke-filled club in Paris,
and he was not afraid.

The Commons

The Bells

We were on Washington Street
at Christmas, all of us,
to look at lights

Nostalgic to say "All of us?"
We were five, each all alone,
clinging to each other and
drifting apart
on those escalator steps

Wet wool and corduroy
and melting snow,
and under that,
worms and impetigo—

Two girls, three boys
looking down at the candy counter
where they kept the non pareils and red hots,
the peanuts heated with a lamp
below us
like a cradle in a manger,
sweet dream of light—

A one-armed hobo
was coming down the escalator
on the other side
as we were going up,
so close we could touch him

—you tried to touch him,
and I slapped your hand—

rags dripping off him
like leaves or shingles
or shitty angel wings,

like something piled up and deep
where sheep would sleep
waiting for a savior and kings.

Boston, 1969

Miscellaneous Opalescence

I am like a pelican in the wilderness, I am like an owl in the desert.

I lie awake, and am like a sparrow on a housetop.

PSALM 102

And I am like a tombstone with a lark etched where a cross should be,
like a book that has been read to death, like a tumbler at the back of a
kitchen cabinet, the last of a set.

In the public gardens, in the fens and in the graveyards, shards of glass
and pottery, billiard and piano keys, bones and insurance policies have
begun to surface, as if New England were trying to speak of plunder, and
of "the suffering that accompanied ivory."

But "after great pain / a formal feeling comes / the nerves sit
ceremonious / like tombs," et cetera. Tombs with snow piled on top, and
a crust of grit on top of that. In Boston the cemeteries come right up
against the highways to vacationland. The enormous Catholic cemeteries,
that is, where thousands of immigrants from Ireland and Italy are buried.

Vast grid of death, no arabesques or grottoes, all of the lanes named
after the saints, and plastic flowers covered in snow propped on the
headstones of the Italians. Nothing Gnostic or ecumenical here, no
God is Love, no doves. *To Jesus Through Mary* is an insinuation when
encountered here among the rows of granite slabs.

A lady in the front office near the gates smokes a cigarette and flicks
through the card file with a dirty lacquered fingernail: "Mary Sullivan,
Mary Sullivan, Mary Sullivan"—there are hundreds of them, cause of
death listed in each case. Servants and mothers, bodies and souls, defiant
girls with secrets hiding among them.

She sends me out into the snow with a map, and I forage among the
Marys, and I am like a daughter looking for an answer from someone

who can never tell. I am a daughter of loss and shame, of defiance, laughter, and a dream of glamour. And my Mary is like an opalescent jar on a windowsill at night—you can't see if she's empty or full.

Heraclitus, from *Cosmic Fragments*: "If all existing things were to become smoke, the nostrils would distinguish them." I smell the blood and smoke in the snow and ice, and I distinguish among all the Marys, and I lay down in the snow.

"For the universe has three children," Emerson wrote, "Jove, Pluto, Neptune . . . or theologically, the Father, the Spirit, and the Son." And one Mother, all Marys.

Across town in another season I wandered in a cemetery like an orchard or a garden, or a book, where New England divines and beneficiaries of the slave trade and abolitionists are buried among Yankees who warned of hordes of papists.

"Went yesterday to Cambridge and spent most of the day at Mount Auburn," Emerson wrote in his journals on April 11, 1834. "I forsook the tombs and found a sunny hollow . . . I heeded no more what minute or hour Massachusetts clocks might indicate."

I walked among the Cabots and the Lodges and stopped at the grave of the botanist Asa Gray, and the yellow leaves fell upon my shoulders as if I were an heir to something, an arboretum, a library, a porch, a problem, a trellis covered with vines of Concord grape. "She does not leave another to baptize her, but baptizes herself."

Tombstones are the covers of books, and there is no rare air, just blood and smoke and a library of bodies and souls. "Genius is the activity which repairs the decay of things."

And I am like the apple I picked and ate there at Mount Auburn that October when the leaves were falling, divinity my compost.

Song of Degrees

I am very much struck in literature by the appearance
that one person wrote all the books . . .

RALPH WALDO EMERSON

In the glare of two-billion-year-old light
these people stand to gain as much as they lose by their position
and they are said to eat their wives and children.
Friends also follow the laws of divine necessity.

The whole frame of things preaches
indifferency. Do not craze yourself with thinking.
The same omniscience flows into the intellect
and makes what we call genius.

They have light and know not whence
it comes. I almost wrote "no not whence,"
and why not wear it thus.

In the nature of the soul is the compensation
for the inequalities of condition. The death
of a brother assumes the aspect of a guide or a genius.
I am my brother and my brother is me.

It has been a luxury to draw the breath
of life. We were children playing with children,
playing with children. You cannot draw the line
where a race begins or ends.
I love a prophet of the soul.

She knew not what to do and so she read.
Having decided what was to be done, she did that.
No matter whether she makes shoes or statues
or laws. It is easy to see

what a favorite she will be with history.
Her book shall smell of pines.

The poets made all the words.
The rainbow, mountains,
orchards in bloom. Stars.

Money is as beautiful as roses.
This is the meaning of their hanging
gardens, villas, garden houses.

Patterns for Arans

We could paint semi-darkness in semi-darkness. And the 'right' lighting
of a picture could be semi-darkness.

WITTGENSTEIN
from *Remarks on Color*

These islands lie off the west coast of Ireland
as if nothing matters.
The people have lived here for centuries
with only a thin covering of soil over the surface.
Great use is made of the seaweed,
the cattle swimming out.

The women here are justly famous.
They weave their own tweed
and make a type of belt called criss.
The heavy Atlantic seas,
the slip stitch.
The difficulty of the patterns
are never written down.

Most impressive and rich, the trellis pattern
and the rope, the tribute to the hardworking bee.
But sometimes their knitting shows mistakes,
with a true Irish touch of nothing
really matters, a careless nonchalance
of the crossing of their cables.

And note mistakes in the simple patterns:
forked lightning or cliff paths,
small fields fenced with stone,
the ups and downs of married life,
the mosses.

The openwork has a religious
significance or none.
Sometimes the clarity of the pattern is
lost through the use of
very fine wool.

Green from the mosses, brown
from the seaweed, grey and cream
color from the stones and pebbles:
many are distinctly over-bobbled.
No matter. They are too lovely
to be lost. Wool and knitting
leaflets can be obtained.

In no case is the whole pattern given.
There are certain gaps and yawns
and part of the pattern is left out
as if it doesn't matter,
or was too lovely,
so was lost.

Some of the simple patterns
are charming for children's jerseys.
This one, for example,
would be lovely on a child.

What Women Won't Waste

The women talking and knitting
watching the guards

The guards spitting

The women knitting
the stares of the guards
into their knitting

Holy Week

A song of degrees, of pilgrimage, as in the Psalms of David

My brothers all have died,
the boys I held when they were small,
when I was small,
the boys I fed and shoved.

Should I lie down with them and keep them warm
or step over them to live?

Or should I crawl across their bodies in pilgrimage
the way my grandmother climbed the concrete steps to the shrine
on her knees, with me one step behind her at her elbow,
her pocketbook swinging at my face
every time she took a step—

In the parlor of her apartment she had a tapestry of the Roman Colosseum
and a crucifix and a picture of Pope John the 23rd
and houseplants in coffee cans on the windowsills—
marvetta, coleus, basilico.

One year after her death at 92, I went to Rome for the first time.
It was Holy Week and all the stores were closed—*chiuso, chiuso, chiuso.*
I was six weeks pregnant.

At the Colosseum I kept stumbling over imaginary statuary,
petrified feet and hands in the grass.
Who died here?

I kneeled to vomit in the weeds.

Fata da forta, my grandmother used to say. Make yourself strong.

I walk around the bodies of my brothers,
arranging their limbs, tracing the contours of their faces
I will remember the clean smell of the grass that grew at the Colosseum
and in the cracks in the steps to the shrine
and I will write about it in a book.

Stanzas in the Form of a Dove

On the way to Yosemite, September 17, 2001, sheep the color of filing
cabinets, wrath on the radio,

religious war—save me, Robert Frost on tape, Groucho Marx, "Your
Show of Shows"—

Men and women in pick-up trucks honking at flags draped from the
overpass near Sacramento

one woman has flags painted on her cheeks—we're boxed in by patriots
and warriors—

Things open up at twilight

we pass rows and rows of trees

uprooted   on their sides   no leaves

an orchard napping

Donald Antrim in the *New Yorker*: "Is the United States now part of the
rest of the world?"

October: Yom Kippur in Oakland. A girl in a T-shirt that says, "By Any
Means Necessary" plays cello

at chapel. Bach, and then we take the children for a walk down to the
lake. We cast our bread upon the

waters. The pelicans glide in to eat our sins. This part of the park smells
like honey.

The morning the World Trade Center was attacked, parents and children
convened at chapel. The

smallest children, mine included, laughed and fooled around in the
pews. No one wanted them to

know what had happened. The eighth graders looked old that morning.

> *Stanzas in the form of a dove —*
> BORGES, from *Invocation to Joyce*

I caught a whiff of Isabel last night, realized she needed a bath. I was so
tired, but I gave her a bath,

helped her with her pajamas, put her to bed. Just before she fell
asleep—I was asleep next to her, I

thought she was asleep—she said, "Mom?"

"Yes?"

"I have a question about being good or bad. I know you should be good,
but if you're not, what can

they do to you? I mean, my question is: Do I always have to be good?"

Does she always have to be good? When I was a girl, I knew I must always be good. Because I was bad.

The filth. Look what original sin has done for me.

So I say to her: "No. You don't always have to *be* good. You *are* good."

She breathes a sigh of relief. "Thank you!" Then falls right to sleep, smelling so sweet.

In the morning I drop her at school, then pass a sign at a gas station:

CLEAN PARTS ARE HAPPY PARTS

The smell of cold hair   cold car   home   I carry her up the stairs

The people downstairs are in love

I can hear them

I have a fever

I put my daughter to bed

breathe her in

and wonder

Those Honeycombs of Light

Men of real religious sense are never shocked.
Christ was never shocked. The Pharisees were shocked.

ALBERTO MORAVIA
(from Pasolini's film, *Love Meetings*)

They found a face separated from a head, they found a kind of treasury
of bones

but these were bones from the meat locker of the restaurant at the top
of the Trade Center

They found

filing cabinets   office supplies   a wig like a scalp   a red shoe   and
steaks and chops

Not the ankles of janitors, the shins of firemen,

just bones that should have ended up on dinner plates

Cold rainy February

The men who dig all day

finish their shift

I watch them leave the pit at night

see women waiting in the shadows

Feast, you who cross the bridge
this cold twilight
on these honeycombs of light, the buildings of Manhattan.

CHARLES REZNIKOFF

The Stars

the daytime

the stars

the waters

the grave

The womb

the arm that hath no strength

the barren   the thing

the mighty

Dead things

the waters

the face

the day and night

THE BOOK OF JOB

The Days

San Francisco, Oakland, New York

Roasting meat, rusting metal, the pavement, the rain,
night

and buses like marionettes cruising through Chinatown
in pink light

My friend from home reads aloud in a café on a hill in San Francisco,
and I hear accents of Creeley and New England

Candles being lit, candles melting in saucers
poets packing up

  Fashion a finger puppet of warm wax

  Fashion a doll

My hallelujah
blots out stars

  .

  Corporate person,
      O!
        Twenty-first-century soul—

The phrase "The Human Bond" is now a piece of corporate property,
it has been trademarked by investment firm Nuveen—

.

The Art Institute is haunted by Irene.

I walk past it in the rain, I think I smell turpentine and I can hear her sepulchral laughter.

I remember her ferocious temper, that outrageous woman, beautiful in her garden, in summer.

She showed us the bread wife she'd made for Craig so he'd have a surrogate while she was out of town. She'd sculpted a vulva from a loaf of bread, glued pubic hair to it—

This was before we had children, before she had one breast removed and reconstructed with a muscle from her back.

"Look," she said, pulling her bathing suit aside to show me as our daughters played at the edge of Lake Anza. "Look what I can do with my new tit—"

And then she flexed it like a bicep

.

Spam:

From Lavern: Exclusive Notice
From Natalie: Attention

If I pay enough attention, will you go away?
Or does it turn you on to be ignored?

These are the little ones that got through the sieve
The little fish—

.

The hand still wants to write 1900 and something though we are finished
with the twentieth century

I have a mitten when a glove is required—

Shit and lavender or holy water
the mother scattering crushed grass, herbs, bitters
around the room
to ward off the stink

This is still happening all over the world,
the world is not new and it still stinks
when it suffers

.

In the sauna at the YMCA, four African American women and me,
reclining on tiled shelves in the heat.

They talk about why they like the Y. One woman says, "I like the diversity,"
and looks at me.

There is general agreement that "die-versity" is a good thing, as are the
new lockers.

The two older women start talking about the little things in life. A nice bed,
a hot plate so you have an option somewhere between the stove and the
microwave. And a porch is a good thing to have, to keep an eye on things.

Discussion about back-in-the-day follows. And talk about shut-ins.

One of them knew someone who was shut in and made Top Ramen every night.

The steam is rising and it's hard to hear—

"Tot Ramen? Like baby food?"

"No, no, Top Ramen. Noodles, you know, with the flavor packet, ten packages for a dollar. I lick that seasoning off my fingers—"

"Oh, TOP Ramen—"

"So this shut-in, she made Top Ramen for herself all hours of the day and night, from her bed, on the hot plate. Never got up, prone all the time, did her business in bed. Found she had a blockage, all that Top Ramen—she couldn't digest it. They had to cut her open."

"Oh what a shame."

Moral: If self-destruction weren't an affordable temptation, it might not be a sin.

.

At Ross Dress for Less, a customer asks the clerk where he should look for sweatpants, and the bored clerk says, "Active bottoms."

"What?" says the incredulous man.

She shouts at him: "ACTIVE BOTTOMS."

Tonight I was playing De La Soul on the CD player on the kitchen counter, listening to "I C Y'all" for the millionth time.

In my high school yearbook I should have been listed as "most likely to annoy her neighbors by playing the same song again and again."

I took the CD out, dropping it accidentally and so neatly into the "one slice" slot of the toaster.

•

> But there is a feeling. A feeling I carry around with me, and that I really want to put at the center of this album. Kind of like folk music, but without any folk attached.
>
> BJÖRK

•

My neighbor is reading a book, *The Ethical Slut*. I saw it on top of the dirty laundry in her basket in the hall last week. I've noticed it in the laundry room before. Is she reading it slowly, or is she re-reading parts, or is it difficult reading?

•

Lots of pelicans diving into and rising out of Lake Merritt this morning. Stopped my bike to watch. Perfectly happy.

On the way home I stop for an egret in the crosswalk.

•

On the porch, outside the poem—

BRIAN TEARE

•

A collage I wasn't able to make for the cover of the chapbook, *There Were Hostilities:* A path of lips cut out of magazines. Pouts like puddingstone. And sulfur and granite: newspaper scraps, headlines, classifieds, bank statements, the NASDAC. *The Human Bond* ™. Pavestones through all kinds of landscapes.

•

The gorgeous young man at the Y, lifting weights, stands with his back to me.

Resting on my back on the nearby bench, I lift my hips slightly, involuntarily, as I remember another man entering me.

This one turns around to rack his weights, and I see he's retarded.

•

The pretty, dark-haired woman in the locker room has waxed her pubic hair all wrong. Or did she pay someone to do this to her?

Poor girl—

A thatch like Charlie Chaplin's mustache sits on her pelvic bone and all the skin above, below, around—
it is unnaturally bare—

The little tramp

·

Old sound of feet on a wooden bridge

New sound of computer saving your work

·

The first suicide ever

The mother who invented the first diaper

The first person ever to break a bottle to use as a weapon

The person who first rhymed two words. Or two sounds. And repeated it again and again.

Anonymous firsts

·

Hauling and *healing*, so close to each other in the *Berkeley Daily Planet* classifieds.

·

I wish my name were Learned Hand. I wish I were so just. And I have wished this for a long time.

·

Booklets

Buckets

Fuck ups

Fightlets

Chocolate

Teddy bears

Even plush toys

Have facets

.

Beautiful meter maid waiting for meters to expire
near Your Black Muslim Bakery:

Bored African goddess

.

I was sitting at my desk thinking of Irene, and a bird sang.

And I thought that was good, that it meant something. Life. Her life, in particular.

And I realized it was also the anniversary of Joseph's death. A long time ago, now.

I wondered why, when birds sing, do we think it is the soul? I mean, I understand why. All poets do. And everyone is a poet when it comes to death.

But is it not the soul, also, when a lizard rustles through dry grass, or when a rotting grapefruit falls from a tree in a parking lot in Oakland, and the birds fly away, startled?

Notes

"Miscellaneous Opalescence"
The lines "After great pain/A formal feeling comes" are from Emily Dickinson's poem 341; "The suffering that accompanied ivory" comes from *Complicity: How the North Promoted, Prolonged, and Profited from Slavery* by Anne Farrow, Joel Lang, and Jenifer Frank. Other sentences in quotation marks come from Ralph Waldo Emerson's writings.

"Song of Degrees"
The title is a reference to the Psalms of David; almost all of the language in this poem comes from the essays of Ralph Waldo Emerson.

"Box of Water" "B Natural" "Sonnet in Search of a Moor" and *"Blood Count"*
These poems draw on factual information found in David Hajdu's biography of Billy Strayhorn.

"The Stars"
The language here is what remains after I erased most of a page of the Book of Job. I took that page from a rain-soaked Bible I found in the wreckage of the Lower Ninth Ward two years after Hurricane Katrina.

"Patterns for Arans"
Most of the phrasing in this poem comes from a knitting manual, *Patterns for Guernseys, Jerseys, and Arans: Fishermen's Sweaters from the British Isles* by Gladys Thompson.

Acknowledgments

The title poem, "The Public Gardens," *Poetry Flash*

"Rose with No Name," "Song of Degrees," and "Holy Week," *Volt*

"Miscellaneous Opalescence," *Shadowbox*

"Box of Water," "B Natural," "Blood Count," *Shuffleboil*

"Sonnet in Search of a Moor," *New American Writing*

"Her Way," *26 Magazine*

Excerpts from "Brooklyn Journals," *Five Fingers Review* and *New American Writing*

"Landscaping for Privacy" and "California," *Mandorla*

"Landscaping for Privacy" has also been set to music by composer Eve Beglarian and is available on her CD *Tell the Birds* and on iTunes.

Some of the poems in this book also appeared in the chapbook *Hesitation Kit* (Etherdome, 2007).

I am grateful to editors and publishers Elizabeth Robinson, Colleen Lookingbill, Maxine Chernoff, Paul Hoover, Tim Roberts, Julie Carr, John-Michael Rivera, Harrison Candelaria Fletcher, Gillian Conoley, Richard Silberg, Joyce Jenkins, Steve Dickison, David Meltzer, Jaime Robles, and Esther Allen; and to the Lannan Foundation (Marfa, 2002). Thank you also to Arthur Goldwag, Susan Moon, Summer Brenner, Carol Snow, Fanny Howe, Michael Russem, and Bill Corbett.

This book is for Isabel Lyndon: "Ah, the luxury of a woman and a girl!"

LINDA NORTON's chapbook, *Hesitation Kit*, was published by Ether-
dome Press in 2007. She has worked in five libraries, three bookstores,
and several publishing houses, including the University of California
Press. She is currently senior editor at The Bancroft Library, University
of California, Berkeley.

She grew up in Boston, spent time in St. Paul and New Haven, lived
in Brooklyn for many years, and now lives in Oakland, California.